Nutritional Cooking with Tofu

Graphique Publishing
Ann Arbor, Michigan

Book design by Jacqueline Sharp

Nutritional Cooking with Tofu

Christine Y.C. Liu

Acknowledgment

A teacher's inspiration comes from one's students, and this is especially true in my case. My students were the inspiration for my previously published books. Their suggestions and feedback have enabled me to share my knowledge of the art of Chinese cuisine more effectively. My thanks go out to colleagues and friends, who in one way or another, encouraged my efforts in writing this third book. Their friendship and confidence have been a constant source of sustenance.

My special thanks go to Jacqueline Sharp who was responsible for book design and descriptive illustrations, to Mrs. Anna Chapekis for her assistance in editing, and the Tofu Factory of Ann Arbor, The Soy Plant for their encouragement and generous supply of Tofu. Thanks also to Mr. Hu Zen Rong of Shanghai Arts and Crafts for his beautiful paper cuttings. My appreciation to Jiang Min Quan for her beautiful calligraphy.

My thanks to my husband Stephen, and our four lovely children. As always, they gave me unconditional support when I needed it most, as well as serving as my final judges for completed recipes.

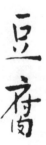

Forward

A whole book of tofu recipes? Why tofu? If you're like us, that's a question that demands an answer. Perhaps you also harbor a mental image of tofu as a tan, gelatinous, and totally tasteless cube, unimaginatively plunked on top of a stir-fried dish or floating in a bowl of thin clear soup. If that's your idea of what tofu is all about, you're in for a big surprise! In fact there isn't a recipe in this whole book that calls for using tofu in such a sterotypical manner.

In this, her third cookbook written for those of us not raised on Chinese cooking, Christine Liu demystifies the art of making delicious tofu-based dishes. Note the choice of words, tofu-based. Properly used, tofu serves as the base or the foundation upon which a startlingly wide variety of delicious dishes can be built. When used in the proper manner, tofu should be viewed as a vehicle to bring flavors together and blend them. In whatever manner it is used, it should not be presented as the source of flavor itself.

If you think this odd, consider the role of cooking oil in your stir-fry dishes or even fried chicken for that matter. If it's good cooking oil, it should be tasteless. Mostly, it serves as a vehicle that permits the flavors of the various ingredients to blend with each other to create a single taste experience. Tofu can play a similar role in the preparation of many dishes, but the story doesn't end there.

Consider some of the other properties of this remarkable substance. You can use it as a thickener like cornstarch, a coating agent like cream, a binder like egg white, or an extender like hamburger helper. Depending on how you mix it, it can come out smooth and creamy, fluffy, crumbly, or stiff. What can you do with all of this? Well, for starters, you can turn this single basic ingredient into a chip or vegetable dip, a salad dressing, a sandwich spread, a dough filling, or a casserole. Talk about versatility!

Still, why should you use tofu for any of these purposes when there are other more familiar ingredients available? Let's look at those ingredients. For the most part, you would have to use cream, sour cream, cheese, starch, or eggs singly or in combination to accomplish all the things tofu can do all by itself. And it is here that tofu's nutritional qualities come into full play.

Not only is tofu low calorie, and virtually cholesterol and sodium free to boot, it is also highly nutritious in its own right as Christine clearly explains in the introductory chapter. It is high in protein, has all the essential amino acids, and is low in fats and carbohydrates. If that weren't enough to recommend it, it is also a wonderful meat substitute for the conscientious vegetarian. Moreover, its' inexpensive price makes it a good addition to the price conscious food budget.

Now a word about the recipes you'll find in this book. Those of you who are acquainted with either of Christine's preceding cookbooks know that all of her recipes are designed for good taste and ease of preparation while remaining true to the finest traditions of Chinese cooking. Accordingly, you will find many time-honored traditional Chinese recipes in this book. Also, to be found here is something of a departure from Christine's earlier recipe collections. In this book you will find greater emphasis on newer Chinese recipes that are currently surfacing in the better restaurants of Taiwan and mainland China. Here you will also find many original creations by Christine herself in a wide range of international cooking traditions.

Only one thing remains to be said. If your guests should ever ask you, "what is it that makes this dish (or dip, spread, etc.) taste so delicious?," you might be better off if you didn't tell them. In the first place, they'll automatically assume it's sinfully rich, they'll never believe there's tofu in it, and they'll be firmly convinced that you're a culinary genius. Of course, they'll be better off if you tell them. Better nutrition, after all, is the most important answer to the question, "why tofu?" But isn't it good to know that there's at least one food where healthful and good eating are the same thing? Thanks again Christine!

Paul Y. Ertel M.D. and Inta J. Ertel, M.D.
Professors
University of Michigan Medical School
Ann Arbor, Michigan

Preface

This is a creative tofu cookbook, with more than half of the recipes lying outside the scope of traditional Chinese tofu dishes. The recipes are the result of creativity and are inspired by many international cooking styles.

In Asia, tofu has been a household food item for hundreds of years. As a result, the Chinese have extensive knowledge about the character of tofu, in terms of usage, versatility, and handling. Therefore even though many of these new dishes were inspired by nonChinese cultures, they are invariably influenced by my Chinese background and tastes.

Because tofu was originally an Asian food, it takes creative and daring people to explore its many alternative uses. You have my congratulations. Enjoy the adventure and have fun!

Library of Congress Number 83-032385
ISBN 0-9610566-8-1

Contents

Introduction

Tofu, or bean curd, is now a fairly common item in the average American supermarket. This high protein, low calorie, low sodium and cholesterol free, versatile and inexpensive food is gaining an increasingly wide following. However, fifteen years ago any mention of tofu would have likely brought blank stares. At that time, interest in health and quality of life was just beginning to affect the majority of the American population. Nevertheless the notion of a rich meat-based diet was still heavily ingrained in our culture.

Fortunately, this trend began to slowly change as Americans began to emphasize quality of life amidst abundance. The great irony of that period was that despite access to great varieties and quantities of food, Americans did not always eat healthily. Heart disease and other physical maladies attributed to diet took a heavy toll on the health of Americans. As a result, quality of food and life took on new importance.

As a trained nutritionist and a teacher of Chinese cooking for over fifteen years, I have been uniquely able to observe this process of change in the attitudes of the public and my students. My first two cookbooks, *Nutrition and Diet With Chinese Cooking*, and *More Nutritional Chinese Cooking*, were designed to meet the new demands of people desirous of eating healthy and delicious food. This new tofu cookbook continues my series of books which emphasize delicious taste and nutritional quality.

Before continuing, a fundamental question needs to be answered, namely "exactly what is tofu?" Well, to begin with, the basic raw material for tofu is soybeans. Soybeans are first ground and blended, water is added, and the mixture is allowed to cook briefly. Then, using a strainer the resulting liquid is squeezed out with much of the raw pulp removed. This soy milk, or "dou jiang," is then mixed with a natural solidifier which results in firm cakes of tofu, ready to be cut and used as desired. This fresh tofu is usually of a smooth off-white color with a gelatinous consistency whose hardness depends on water content.

Of course, tofu is a uniquely Asian food, with roots of almost 2,000 years in China. In China, people have known intuitively for centuries that soybeans are an important source of protein. In a country with an historical overpopulation problem and limited land resources, a heavily meat-based diet was both impractical and unfeasible. The typical image of a Chinese peasant toiling in a field amid rich greenery rather than tending a grazing herd of livestock is not without its rationale. We now know that soybeans produce over 33% more protein from an acre of land than other known crops and 20 times as much protein than an acre of land used for grazing cattle or fodder. In fact, soybeans contain 34%-37% protein, which makes them the best source of vegetable protein in the world, with the exception of a few obscure plants. Moreover, for a protein source to be completely available to the body, it must contain amounts of each of the eight essential amino acids in a form readily usable by our bodies.

It is clear then that the the basic raw material for tofu is a highly nutritious, high quality and inexpensive protein source. For our body's metabolism, there is essentially no difference between plant and animal proteins in terms of nutritional use. However, meat extracted protein is often associated with high cholesterol and saturated fats. Soybean foods such as tofu contain no cholesterol, are very low in saturated fats, and are low in calories. It is precisely because of these facts, its low price and high quality, that I call tofu and other soybean based items, the "food of the future."

The soybean originated, most agronomists agree, somewhere in Northern China, where the heavy summer rainfall suits the growing plant. It is said that Emperor Sheng-nung first described the soybean in 2838 B.C. However, the first reliable historical references are dated several thousand years later. A later ruler, Liu An, is credited with creating the technique of making tofu as early as the second century B.C. From that time, the Chinese have turned tofu cooking into a wide-ranging variety of dishes, spanning each of the regional schools. This was made possible because tofu is essentially neutral in taste.This neutrality of taste which so many Westerners find so unappealing, is precisely what gives rise to tofu's amazing versatility of use. Of course, plain tofu is unappealing! All food is this way when preparation is done without using one's imagination.

This book takes the traditional Chinese versatility in tofu preparation, and extends it to cover a much wider area. This entails a considerable use of imagination and inventiveness in creating new recipes. All of the recipes revolve around that most Asian of ingredients—tofu. However, as you try the various recipes, you will find the results range from the familiar to the exotic and international. The techniques and styles are not confined to China or Asia. Like my earlier well received books, each of the recipes also contains detailed nutritional information for each recipe.

Using the nutritional information makes it possible for those on controlled and vegetarian diets to plan a well-balanced menu. Indeed, tofu is an ideal diet and vegetarian food. A typical eight-ounce serving contains only approximately 150 calories. An equal weight of eggs contains two times as many calories, and an equal weight of beef, four to five times as many. In China, tofu is a major source of protein in the diet and cross-cultural studies have shown that the incidence of serious heart disease is less frequent there. Americans have one of the worst diets in the world with respect to cholesterol and saturated fats. Myths persist that meats contain more quality protein than any food, or that eating meat is the only way to get enough protein. These beliefs are simply not true, and our health demands that alternative sources of protein such as tofu, be utilized and popularized. In addition to being high in protein content, tofu is also rich in minerals and vitamins, containing significant amounts of calcium, iron, phosphorus, and vitamins B and E.

The use of tofu as a healthy source of protein in the diet is appealing by its many aforementioned attributes and qualities. Furthermore, its consumption can be viewed in much wider perspective. Agronomists and agricultural specialists now agree that the world will soon face a serious protein shortage. Increasing world population and declining areas of readily arable land makes this an important issue on the world's future agenda. Because of the soybeans high quality and quantity of protein, it is viewed as one of the essential weapons to fight this threat. The United States is the worlds largest producer of soybeans, most of which we export to Western Europe and Japan. Yet the portion that we retain is processed into various food oils and agents which find their way into our processed foods as subsidiary elements. A still greater portion of this is ground and fed to our livestock for the production of meat. The result is that from an ecological and health perspective, one highly desirable protein is given to livestock to produce what is in many ways a less healthy food.

Essentially then, a meat-centered diet represents a waste of the earth's resources. Tofu use is now becoming popular because it is beginning to make plain good sense to us in terms of health and nutrition. With the continuously rising price of meat and our increasing vulnerability to the needs of the world-food system as a whole, it makes equally good sense.

The recipes in this book were designed with simplicity and good taste in mind. Almost all of the ingredients in the recipes are readily available in the average American supermarket. And for goodness sakes, if your grocer doesn't carry tofu, encourage him to do so. I hope that the wide variety of dishes, desserts, soups, salads, salad dressings, and dips in this book will provide you with many occasions for delicious and healthful eating.

Nutritional Values

Each recipe in this book is accompanied by a list of the nutritional values. **These values are calculated for each serving.** Included in the nutritional lists are the number of calories; grams of protein, carbohydrates, fat (the percentage of saturated fat is also included), and fiber; milligrams of cholesterol (despite the fact that many recipes are cholesterol free), sodium, and calcium.

Nutritional values used in the calculations are based on a computer program: The Food Processor II, by ESHA research, U.S. Department of Agriculture information, and nutritional text books. The values are inclusive for all ingredients listed, but do not reflect substitutions or optional ingredients. If the recipes are listed with one or more alternative ingredient, the first item or measurement is used to calculate the nutritional value.

Fat

Fat is one of the very important ingredients in cooking. It is also an essential nutrient that is necessary for good health and growth. But fats, as one of the major food groups, is linked to obesity, heart disease and certain cancers when too much, or the wrong kind, is consumed.

Generally speaking, there are two types of fat. Both of them are made up of a mixture of saturated fat and unsaturated (polyunsaturated and monounsaturated) fat.

Fat which is liquid at room temperature is referred to as oil. Oils are found predominantly in foods of plant origin such as safflower, sunflower, corn, soybean, peanut, canola (rape seed), sesame, etc. They contain no cholesterol and have a fair amount of unsaturated fat. Unsaturated fats have the capacity of lowering the blood cholesterol level. Recent research indicates that while both polyunsaturated and monounsaturated fats lower **total** blood cholesterol, monounsaturated fats do not lower the protective (HDL) cholesterol as do polyunsaturated fats. The use of monounsaturated fats, therefore, is encouraged.

Fat which is solid at room temperature is referred to simply as fat. Fats are found predominantly in foods of animal origin such as lard, butter, chicken fat, etc. They contain cholesterol and are found mostly in saturated fats. A diet high in saturated fat tends to raise the cholesterol level of the blood. People should use them with discrimination.

3

In this book, vegetable oils are used for all the recipes. All types of vegetable oils are recommended (except coconut and palm oils) for use in cooking. Vegetable oils are cholesterol free and high in both polyunsaturated and monounsaturated fats. Corn oil was used for all the calculations of nutritional values. The use of peanut oil, which is higher in monounsaturated fat, and canola oil (pages 5 and 162) which is lowest in saturated fat, is encouraged by anyone who has high blood cholesterol and other related health problems.

Sodium

A great attention has been given to the sodium content of food recently. This has been the result of evidence that excess sodium in the diet contributes to high blood pressure (also known as hypertension) in some people. In turn, high blood pressure has been identified as a significant contributor to cardiovascular and renal disease.

Recent research conducted by the Michigan Heart Association revealed some startling facts: one in every four adults has high blood pressure, yet 75% of those do not have it under control. To control sodium intake from food and drinks, as well as drugs prescribed by physicians, is one of the methods used to control high blood pressure.

No one denies that man needs sodium. It is an essential nutrient which is necessary for the body to regulate blood pressure and blood volume. It is also needed for nerves and muscles to function well. However, the need is very small. An intake of 1,100-3,200 milligrams per day is considered safe and adequate. Most dietary sodium is found in salt. One teaspoon of salt contains approximately 2,000 milligrams of sodium.

Many Americans consume about 2-7 grams of sodium per day (equivalent to 1-3 teaspoons of salt); clearly more than they need. To meet the needs of the public's greater sensitivity to sodium intake, I have calculated the sodium content of every recipe. For those on sodium restricted diets, the sodium content calculated can be further reduced by using low sodium products as substitutes such as low sodium soy sauce, barbecue sauce and canned foods, etc. I hope that these special calculations will bring you greater convenience in planning your menus as well as healthful eating.

Definition of Terms

Cholesterol is a fatty substance that is made in the body and carried in the blood. It is only present in foods of animal origin. Every 1% reduction in serum cholesterol results in a 2% reduction in risk for coronary artery disease.

HDL cholesterol is that portion carried in the blood most highly associated with a low incidence of coronary artery disease.

LDL cholesterol is that portion carried in the blood most highly associated with a high incidence of coronary artery disease.

Triglyceride is a fat in the blood made from foods we eat. Triglycerides are made from fat, alcohol, sugar, and when too many calories are consumed.

Calories are units of energy. Protein, carbohydrate, fat, and alcohol are all sources of energy.

Protein is a substance needed by every cell for building body tissue. In order for this to occur, calories adequate to meet minimum energy needs must be consumed.

Carbohydrate is the general term for sugars and starches. Carbohydrate is necessary as an energy source.

Fat is found in foods of both plant and animal origin. It is an important source of energy in our diets and carries some vitamins.

Water soluble fiber is found in oat bran, dried beans, barley, oats, buckwheat, vegetables, and fruits. It helps reduce LDL cholesterol levels.

Polyunsaturated fat is a fat usually found in foods of plant origin. Many liquid oils are polyunsaturated. The oils highest in polyunsaturated fats are safflower, sunflower, corn and soybean, in that order.

Monounsaturated fat is found in both plant and animal foods. Those highest in monounsaturated fat are canola (rape seed) oil, olive oil, avocado, peanut butter and most nuts.

Saturated fat is a fat found in foods of both animal and vegetable origin. Examples of vegetable sources of saturated fat are coconut oil, palm oil, and vegetable shortening that has been hydrogenated (made solid).

P/S Ratio is the ratio of polyunsaturated fats to saturated fats. The higher the P/S ratio of a fat or oil, the more effective it will be in lowering the blood cholesterol level.

Tips on Keeping and Using Tofu

- Always immerse tofu in cold water and store in a refrigerator.

- Change water at least once every two days. Tofu can be kept for 10 days.

- Fried Tofu (page 157) can be kept a week in the refrigerator or a few months in the freezer. Fried Tofu can be added to soups, casseroles, and braised dishes. It can also be stuffed with ground meat, vegetables, and mashed, seasoned tofu.

- Soft tofu is good in soups and dishes with gravy. Firmer tofu is good in stir-fry dishes. Both types are exchangeable depending on personal preference. Most of the tofu sold in supermarkets is the firmer type because it is easy to handle and ship.

- Tofu dishes taste best when warm or hot.

- Tofu dishes reheat well.

- Tofu can be frozen. Freezing will change the texture of tofu into a spongy consistency. It is more chewy than regular tofu. Thaw and squeeze out the water before using.

- Dry tofu, or Tofu Gan (page 157) freezes well. Freezing will not change dry tofu's texture. Sliced or shredded Tofu Gan stir-fries well with vegetables and meat.

- Tofu can be added to any of your favorite dishes. It absorbs the flavor of other ingredients easily and adds good protein to your diet.

- Most tofu dishes require a very short cooking time. Use it as an emergency food which can be easily added to your menu.

- Tofu contains no cholesterol and is very low in sodium. It is an ideal food for those on cholesterol and sodium restricted diets.

- Tofu's high quality protein and low calorie characteristics make it an ideal food for dieters.

- Tofu is inexpensive and easily digested. It is good for people of all walks of life and all ages.

- Tofu is high in unsaturated fat and low in saturated fat. Saturated fat in one pound of tofu is only 8%.

- Tofu is high in calcium. One pound of tofu contains 476 mg of calcium.

soup

湯

SOUP

HOT AND SOUR TOFU SOUP

Ingredients:

⅛ lb	shredded pork
4 t	low sodium instant chicken or vegetable bouillon
½ lb	firm or soft tofu, shredded
4 C	water
1 t	cornstarch
1 T	low sodium or regular soy sauce
½ C	washed, soaked and shredded dried wood ears
15	dried lily buds, washed and soaked
1-2	Chinese dried mushrooms, washed and soaked
¼ C	bamboo shoots, shredded
½ lb	firm or soft tofu, shredded
4 T	vinegar
2 T	cornstarch blended with 4 T water
2	egg whites, lightly beaten
1 t	sesame oil
¼ t	pepper
1 t	Hot Pepper Sauce (page 92) (optional)
1-2	green onion, minced

Method:

1. Mix pork with 1 T soy sauce and 1 t cornstarch. Set aside.
2. Soak lily buds, wood ears and mushroom in separate small bowls of hot water for 40 minutes.
3. Cut mushrooms into shreds; wash wood ears thoroughly; have the lily buds drained and knotted (see next page), and the bamboo shoots ready.
4. Put 4 C of water and the 4 t instant bouillon in a medium saucepan and bring to a boil.
5. Add pork, mushroom, wood ears, lily buds, and bamboo shoots. Bring to a boil again.
6. Add tofu shreds; bring to a boil once more.
7. Stir in 4 T vinegar and 2 T blended cornstarch. Cook until the soup thickens.
8. Turn off heat. Stir in beaten egg whites and 1 t sesame oil. Add Hot Pepper Sauce (if desired), and ¼ t pepper.

9. Pour into a tureen. Sprinkle minced green onion on the surface of the soup. Serve hot. Makes 6 servings.

Per serving:

Calories: 85	Fat: 4 gm (saturated fat = 4%)
Carbohydrates: 7 gm	Cholesterol: 7 mg
Protein: 6 gm	Sodium: 125 mg
Fiber: 1 gm	Calcium: 47 mg

MUSHROOM TOFU SOUP

Ingredients:

½ lb	firm or soft tofu, sliced (2"x1"x½")
¼ lb	lean pork butt or chicken breast, sliced (1"x1"x⅛")
1 T	low sodium or regular soy sauce
⅛ t	onion or garlic powder
⅛ t	pepper
1 t	sherry
1 t	cornstarch
3 t	low sodium instant chicken or vegetable bouillon
3 C	water
3	slices of ginger root
¼ lb	mushrooms, sliced
¼-½ C	sliced bamboo shoots
¼ lb	or more, celery cabbage or spinach, cut into ½" pieces
1 C	frozen peas (optional)
1 t	sesame oil (optional)

Continued on next page

Method:

1. Mix meat with the next 5 ingredients. Set aside.
2. Place the chicken or vegetable bouillon in a saucepan. Add the next 4 ingredients; cover and bring to a boil.
3. Add meat slices one by one; bring to a boil.
4. Add tofu slices; bring to a boil.
5. Add rest of the ingredients and bring to a boil. Pour the soup into a tureen; sprinkle with sesame oil and serve hot.

This soup can be thickened with 1 T blended cornstarch before serving. Makes 6 servings.

Per serving:

Calories: 107	Fat: 5 gm (saturated fat = 3%)
Carbohydrates: 8 gm	Cholesterol: 13 mg
Protein: 9 gm	Sodium: 137 mg
Fiber: 3 gm	Calcium: 60 mg

BEAN THREAD FRIED TOFU SOUP

Ingredients:

2 oz	bean thread (dried form, in packages)
10	Chinese dried mushrooms or ¼ lb fresh mushrooms
4 oz	Fried Tofu* (page 157)
2-3 t	low sodium instant chicken or vegetable bouillon
½ C	sliced bamboo shoots
6 C	water (including the water from soaking dried mushrooms)
4	or more, slices of ginger root
½ t	pepper
1 T	sherry
2	green onions, minced
1 T	sesame oil
	Salt or soy sauce to taste

Method:

1. Soak the bean thread in hot water for 15 minutes; drain and cut into 2" sections.
2. Soak the Chinese mushrooms in hot water for 1 hour or until soft; drain but reserve the water. Discard mushroom stems and cut mushrooms into halves.
3. Place all the ingredients, except green onions and sesame oil, in a large saucepan; cover and bring to a boil. Reduce to low heat and simmer for 20 minutes.
4. Sprinkle green onions and sesame oil on the soup before serving. Serve hot. Makes 6 servings.

Fish balls, (fresh or frozen ones are sold in Oriental grocery stores), or meat balls may be added to this soup.

*Fried Tofu is also available in Oriental grocery stores.

Per serving:

Calories: 115   Fat: 5 gm (saturated fat = 6%)
Carbohydrates: 12 gm   Cholesterol: 0 mg
Protein: 6 gm   Sodium: 7 mg
Fiber: 2 gm   Calcium: 48 mg

CUSTARD TOFU SOUP

Ingredients:

1 C	coagulated soy milk (step 8 of the recipe for making tofu, page 152; sodium sulfate is used as coagulant)
1 T	minced Sichuan pickle
1 T	low sodium or regular soy sauce
1 T	soaked and minced dried shrimp or minced ham
1 T	minced green onion
1 t	sesame oil
1 t	Red Hot Pepper Oil (page 90)
	Pinch of pepper

Continued on next page

Method:

1. Place 1 C coagulated soy milk in a Chinese rice bowl or soup bowl.
2. Add the rest of the ingredients. Serve hot. Mix before eating. Makes 2 servings.

Per serving:

Calories: 130	Fat: 9 gm (saturated fat = 9%)
Carbohydrates: 4 gm	Cholesterol: 3 mg
Protein: 12 gm	Sodium: 468 mg
Fiber: 2 gm	Calcium: 142 mg

SEAWEED SOUP

Ingredients:

4 t	low sodium instant bouillon dissolved in 4 C hot water, 4 C soup broth, or 4 C homemade broth (page 16)
1 lb	firm or soft tofu sliced into 1"x½"x⅛" slices
1-2 oz	seaweed sheets (Zhi Cai), (see page 164)
1 t	cornstarch blended with 2 T water
2	green onions, minced
1 T	sesame oil
¼ t	pepper
	A few spinach leaves or vegetables of your choice (optional)

Method:

1. Place the broth in a saucepan and bring to a boil.
2. Add tofu slices and bring to a boil.
3. Break the seaweed into small pieces. Add the seaweed and the rest of the ingredients and cook until the soup thickens. Serve hot. Makes 6 servings.

Per serving:

Calories: 93	Fat: 6 gm (saturated fat = 8%)
Carbohydrates: 5 gm	Cholesterol: 0 mg
Protein: 6 gm	Sodium: 20 mg
Fiber: 1 gm	Calcium: 89 mg

VELVET CORN SOUP

Ingredients:

10 oz	frozen cut corn, thawed, or corn from fresh ears
½ lb	soft or firm tofu
4 t	low sodium instant chicken or vegetable bouillon, or 3 C canned broth
3 C	water
1 C	skim milk
2 T	cornstarch dissolved in ¼ C water
2	egg whites, lightly beaten
1 oz	minced ham (optional)
1-2	green onions, minced
	Salt and pepper to taste

Method:

1. Place the corn, chicken or vegetable bouillon, and tofu in a blender or a food processor. Blend for 1-2 minutes.
2. Pour the corn mixture in a saucepan; add milk and water, and bring to a boil.
3. Add dissolved cornstarch, stirring constantly until the soup thickens.
4. Remove from heat; fold in egg whites.
5. Pour into a tureen. Sprinkle minced onion, ham, and a little salt and pepper on the soup. Serve hot. Makes 6 servings.

One half to one teaspoon of sesame oil can be added before serving.

Per serving:

Calories: 77
Carbohydrates: 16 gm
Protein: 4 gm
Fiber: 2 gm

Fat: 0.125 gm (saturated fat = 6%)
Cholesterol: 0.667 mg
Sodium: 44 mg
Calcium: 54 mg

HOMEMADE BROTH

Ingredients:

5 lb	cut up fryer, hen or stewing chicken for chicken broth, or beef stew meat and bones for beef broth
2 in	ginger root, crushed
1	onion, quartered
4-6 qt	cold water

Method:

Place all the ingredients in a large saucepan or dutch oven; cover and bring slowly to a boil. Remove scum; cover and simmer over low heat for a few hours (2-5). Strain, chill, and remove fat. The broth is now ready for your favorite soups. Add salt, soy sauce, and pepper to adjust the flavor before using. The long, slow cooking extracts all the flavor and nutrients from the meat and bones. The Chinese use homemade broth as a basic ingredient for their cooking. Part of the calcium in their daily diet is furnished by the broth.

Nutritional information for homemade broth is not available.

TOFU SOUP

Ingredients:

½ lb	firm or soft tofu, sliced (2"x1"x½")
¼ lb	lean pork or chicken breast, sliced (2"x1"x⅛")
1 T	low sodium or regular soy sauce
⅛ t	onion powder
⅛ t	pepper
1 t	cornstarch
3 t	low sodium instant chicken or vegetable bouillon dissolved in 3 C water, or 3 C homemade chicken broth (page 16), or 3 C canned broth
2	slices of ginger root (optional)
¼ lb	celery cabbage or spinach, cut into 1" sections

Method:

1. Mix pork (or chicken breast) with the next 4 ingredients. Set aside.
2. Put the chicken broth and ginger root in a deep saucepan; bring to a boil.
3. Add the tofu slices; bring to a boil.
4. Add the meat slices one by one and bring to a boil.
5. Add the vegetables and again bring to a boil. Add sesame oil and serve hot. Makes 6 servings.

Per serving:

Calories: 75	Fat: 4 gm (saturated fat = 3%)
Carbohydrates: 4 gm	Cholesterol: 13 mg
Protein: 7 gm	Sodium: 109 mg
Fiber: 1 gm	Calcium: 54 mg

BOILED TOFU BALL SOUP

Ingredients:

3 t   low sodium instant chicken or vegetable bouillon dissolved in 3 C hot water, or 3 C homemade chicken broth (page 16), or 3 C canned broth

½ C   sliced bamboo shoots or sliced water chestnuts (or both)

½ C   sliced mushrooms

Few spinach, napa or bok choy leaves, cut into small pieces

1 t   sesame oil

Tapioca powder for coating

Continued on next page

Soup

¼ lb	ground pork, beef or minced shrimp
2	green onions, minced
1 t	finely minced ginger root
¼ t	pepper
1 t	sherry
2 T	low sodium or regular soy sauce
4	water chestnuts, coarsely minced
1 t	sesame oil
½ lb	firm tofu, crumbled
½ t	garlic powder
2 T	tapioca

Method:

1. Place the last 11 ingredients in a bowl and mix thoroughly.
2. Form the tofu mixture into 1" balls. Roll each ball in a layer of tapioca; press to coat. Makes 18-21 balls.
3. Place the first 3 ingredients in a saucepan and bring to a boil. Add tofu balls; stir carefully and continue to boil.
4. Add ½ C of water, reduce to low heat and bring to a boil.
5. Add vegetables and bring to a boil.
Serve immediately. Makes 6 servings.

Per serving:

Calories: 133	Fat: 7 gm (saturated fat = 3%)
Carbohydrates: 6 gm	Cholesterol: 27 mg
Protein: 11 gm	Sodium: 207 mg
Fiber: 1 gm	Calcium: 54 mg

DUMPLING SOUP

Ingredients:

½	recipe of Fluffy Tofu (page 72) as dumpling filling
1	recipe homemade dumpling wrappers (below)
	Minced green onions, sesame oil and minced cilantro for garnishing
	Instant vegetable or chicken bouillon (1 t dissolved in 1 C hot water), or homemade broth (page 16)
	Salt and pepper to taste

Recipe for Homemade Dumpling Wrappers

Ingredients:

　1 ¼ C　all purpose flour
　　½ C　water

Method:

　Mix flour and water in a mixing bowl to form a dough. Knead the dough on a floured board for 7-8 minutes, or until soft and smooth. Form the dough into a sausage-like, cylindrical roll, about 1" in diameter. Cut the roll, crosswise into 20 pieces. Flatten each piece of dough with the palm of your hand and with a rolling pin, roll out into a round wrapper about 2-2½" in diameter. See photo on page 20, step 1.

Method for Wrapping Dumplings and Preparing Soup:

1. Place a portion (approximately 1 teaspoonful) of the fluffy tofu in the center of the wrapper. Moisten the edges with a little water. Fold the wrapper in half across the filling. Pinch the edges to seal. (Or follow instructions on pages, 21-22, steps, 2-5).
2. Boil 2-3 cups of broth or bouillon in a pan. Keep hot.
3. To cook the dumplings: Fill a large deep saucepan one-third full of water; bring to a boil. Carefully drop the 20 dumplings into the boiling water; stir gently to prevent sticking. Cover and bring to a boil. Add 1 cup of cold water; cover, and bring to a boil once more. Remove the cooked dumplings with a slotted spoon into a tureen. Add the hot broth to cover the dumplings. Garnish with green onions, sesame oil, and cilantro. Serve hot. Makes 20 dumplings.

Tips:

- Do not cook too many dumplings at one time.

- A few vegetable leaves can be added to the broth to increase the nutritional value of the soup. The vegetables will also make the soup more colorful and appetizing.

Continued on next page

- The stuffings for Curried and Spinach Strudels (pages 106-107) can also be used as dumpling fillings.

- This soup can be served as a snack, lunch, or as a meal.

Each dumpling:

Calories: 38
Carbohydrates: 5 gm
Protein: 2 gm
Fiber: 0.4 gm

Fat: 1 gm (saturated fat = 4%)
Cholesterol: 0 mg
Sodium: 51 mg
Calcium: 15 mg

Wrapping Dumplings:

1. Roll dough pieces into 2½" wrappers.

2. Place 1 teaspoon of filling in the center of a dumpling wrapper.

3. Fold the wrapper in half across the filling and pinch once in the center.

4. Make 3 or 4 pleats on one side of the center; repeat on other side, shaping the dumpling into a 3-sided crescent shape.

5. Pinch the edges along the pleated side in order to seal tightly.

Photographs by Sheryl White

WONTON SOUP

Ingredients:

20   wrapped wontons (use the Fried Wonton recipe on
     page 136, steps 1-3)
     Minced green onions, sesame oil, and minced cilantro
     for garnishing.
     Homemade broth (page 16), canned chicken or beef
     broth or, instant bouillon (1 t dissolved in 1 C hot
     water)
     Salt and pepper or soy sauce to taste

To Cook and Serve:

Follow step 3 of Dumpling Soup recipe (page 19).

Each uncooked wonton:

Calories: 20   Fat: 1 gm (saturated fat = 4%)
Carbohydrates: 3 gm   Cholesterol: 0 mg
Protein: 1 gm   Sodium: 18 mg
Fiber: 0.4 gm   Calcium: 14 mg

Wrapping Wontons:

1. Put ½ teaspoon of filling in the center of a wonton skin (wrapper).

2. Fold the wrapper in half toward you (with the filling in the center).

3. Fold the wrapper in half once more in the same direction.

Photographs by Sheryl White

4. Holding the two corners of the center fold (leaving the two bottom corners free), pull forward. Overlap the corners, moisten and press to seal.

5. Wontons should have the appearance of little nurse's caps.

main dishes

MAIN DISHES-With Small Portion of Meat

Bear's Palm Tofu, 41
Black Bean Tofu with Meat Sauce, 32
Braised Fried Tofu with Shrimp, 38
Braised Tofu in Meat Sauce, 33
Fermented Tofu (Tofu Lu) with Meat, 51
Honey Comb Tofu, 34
Hot Tofu, 50
Ma La Tofu, 42
Ma Po Tofu, 47
Meat-Stuffed Fried Tofu, 36
Meat with Tofu Gan, 48
Shrimp Tofu, 44
Sichuan Tofu, 40
Tofu Foo Young, 37
Tofu Meat Balls, 45
Tofu with Assorted Meats and Vegetables, 31
Tofu with Bamboo Shoots, 46
Tofu with Chicken, 30
Tofu with Fish in Earthenware Pot, 49
Tofu with Ham, 35
Tofu with Pickled Greens, 39
Tofu with Smoked Fish, 43

TOFU WITH CHICKEN

Ingredients:

1 lb	firm tofu, sliced (2"x1"x½")
1 T	low sodium or regular soy sauce
2 t	cornstarch
¼ lb	chicken breast
½ lb	or more, bok choy
½ lb	or more, tomatoes, cubed
2-3 T	corn or canola oil
2	or more, green onions, shredded
2	slices of ginger root
2-3 T	low sodium or regular soy sauce
¼ t	pepper
⅛ t	sugar
	Salt to taste
1 t	sesame oil (optional)

Method:

1. Wash the bok choy and cut into 1" sections. Separate the white parts from the green parts. Set aside.

2. Slice the chicken and mix it with 1 T soy sauce and 2 t cornstarch.

3. Heat oil in a **nonstick** pan or wok; sauté onions and ginger root. Add meat and stir-fry for 1-2 minutes.

4. Add tofu, the white parts of the bok choy, tomatoes, and the last 5 ingredients; bring to a boil.

5. Add the green parts of the bok choy and cook over high heat for one minute. Serve hot. Makes 6 servings.

Per serving:

Calories: 141
Carbohydrates: 6 gm
Protein: 12 gm
Fiber: 2 gm

Fat: 9 gm (saturated fat = 7%)
Cholesterol: 11 mg
Sodium: 324 mg
Calcium: 124 mg

TOFU WITH ASSORTED MEATS AND VEGETABLES

Ingredients:

1 lb	firm tofu, cut into 1"x2"x½" slices
2-3 T	corn or canola oil
2	slices of ginger root
2	green onions, shredded
½ t	low sodium or regular salt
4	Chinese dried mushrooms
1-2 t	low sodium instant chicken or vegetable bouillon
½ C	sliced bamboo shoots
¼ lb	shelled shrimp, fresh or frozen
¼ lb	pork loin, sliced
1 t	cornstarch
2 t	sherry (divided)
1 T	low sodium or regular soy sauce
⅛ t	pepper
2 t	cornstarch blended with ¼ C of water
1 t	sesame oil

Method:

1. Soak mushrooms in 1 C of hot water for 1 hour; squeeze out excess water and cut each mushroom into four pieces. Save the mushroom water for later use.
2. Mix shrimp with 1 t sherry, ⅛ t salt and 1 t cornstarch. Mix the pork slices with the same amount of seasoning. Set aside.
3. Heat oil in a **nonstick** pan or wok; add onions, ginger, and tofu slices. Spread ½ t salt evenly on tofu. Lightly brown both sides of the tofu.
4. Add the mushroom water, mushrooms, chicken or vegetable bouillon, and bamboo shoot slices; bring to a boil.
5. Add shrimp and meat slices one by one to the pan; stir and mix for 1 minute.
6. Add soy sauce and pepper; bring to a boil. Stir in the blended cornstarch and sesame oil; cook until the sauce thickens.
Serve hot. Makes 6 servings.

Continued on next page

Per serving:

Calories: 174	Fat: 11 gm (saturated fat = 6%)
Carbohydrates: 6 gm	Cholesterol: 37 mg
Protein: 14 gm	Sodium: 226 mg
Fiber: 2 gm	Calcium: 100 mg

BLACK BEAN TOFU WITH MEAT SAUCE

Ingredients:

1 lb	firm or soft tofu, diced
2	green onions, minced
2	thin slices of ginger root, minced
3 T	fermented (salted) black beans, finely chopped (see page 162)
⅛ lb	ground lean pork or beef
2-3 T	corn or canola oil
⎧ 2 T	low sodium or regular soy sauce
⎨ ⅛ t	pepper
⎩ ¼ t	sugar

Method:

1. Heat oil in a **nonstick** pan or wok; sauté the onions and ginger root.
2. Add meat and fermented (salted) black beans. Stir-fry for 2 minutes.
3. Add tofu dices and the last 3 ingredients. Mix and bring to a boil; stir while cooking. Serve hot. Makes 6 servings.

Per serving:

Calories: 131	Fat: 10 gm (saturated fat = 8%)
Carbohydrates: 3 gm	Cholesterol: 7 mg
Protein: 10 gm	Sodium: 293 mg
Fiber: 1 gm	Calcium: 96 mg

BRAISED TOFU IN MEAT SAUCE

Ingredients:

¼ lb	lean ground meat, pork or beef
1 T	low sodium or regular soy sauce
¼ t	onion powder
⅛ t	pepper
1 t	sherry
1 t	cornstarch
1 lb	firm or soft tofu
¼ t	low sodium or regular salt
2-3 T	corn or canola oil
2	green onions, minced
1 t	minced ginger root
1 T	minced garlic
1-3 t	Hot Pepper Sauce (page 92)
2 t	cornstarch blended with 2 T water
½ t	low sodium instant chicken or vegetable bouillon
1 C	water
1 t	sugar

Method:

1. Mix the meat with the next 5 ingredients. Set aside.
2. Cut the tofu into 1½"x½" squares, then cut the squares into triangles.
3. Heat oil in a **nonstick** pan or wok; put the tofu triangles in the pan. Sprinkle ⅓ t salt evenly over the tofu.
4. Fry the tofu until brown. Brown the other side. Remove.
5. Add meat, ginger, garlic and Hot Pepper Sauce; stir and mix for 1 minute. Add the last 3 ingredients; bring to a boil.
6. Add cooked tofu; cook for 4-5 minutes. Add blended cornstarch and cook until the sauce thickens. Transfer to a serving dish and sprinkle the minced green onions over the tofu. Serve hot. Makes 6 servings.

Per serving:

Calories: 145	Fat: 10 gm (saturated fat = 7%)
Carbohydrates: 5 gm	Cholesterol: 13 mg
Protein: 10 gm	Sodium: 167 mg
Fiber: 1 gm	Calcium: 89 mg

HONEY COMB TOFU

Ingredients:

1 lb	firm or soft tofu, frozen
½ lb	chicken breast
⅛ t	low sodium or regular salt
¼ t	pepper
½ t	onion powder
1 t	sherry
2 t	cornstarch
1 t	low sodium instant chicken or vegetable bouillon
1 t	cornstarch blended with 1 T water
1 T	sesame oil
3 T	chopped coriander for garnishing
2-3 T	corn or canola oil
2	green onions, shredded
3	slices ginger root
⅛ lb	fresh mushrooms, washed and sliced
⅛ lb	snow pea pods, washed and cleaned
1 C	or more, water
2 t	low sodium instant chicken or vegetable bouillon
1 T	low sodium or regular soy sauce
1 oz	sliced ham (optional)

Method:

1. Pat the tofu dry. Keep in in the freezer overnight or longer. Thaw completely and cut into 2"x1"x½" pieces before using.
2. Slice the chicken then mix with the next 6 ingredients.
3. Heat oil in a **nonstick** pan or wok; sauté onion and ginger root. Add chicken and stir for 1 minute.
4. Add tofu and the last 4 ingredients; bring to a boil.
5. Add mushrooms and pea pods; bring to a boil.
6. Add blended cornstarch and cook until the sauce thickens. Transfer to a serving dish. Garnish with sesame oil and chopped coriander. Serve hot. Makes 6 servings.

After fresh tofu has been frozen, holes appear which gives it the appearance of honey comb. The spongy character soaks up flavor easily. It is also the best way to use up any surplus fresh tofu.

Per serving:

Calories: 165	Fat: 9 gm (saturated fat = 7%)
Carbohydrates: 6 gm	Cholesterol: 22 mg
Protein: 16 gm	Sodium: 156 mg
Fiber: 2 gm	Calcium: 94 mg

TOFU WITH HAM

Ingredients:

½ lb	firm or soft tofu, sliced (2"x1"x½")
2-3 T	corn or canola oil
2	green onions, shredded
2	slices of ginger root
¼ lb	ham, sliced (2"x1"x⅙")
½ lb	bok choy
½ lb	fresh tomatoes, cut into cubes
2-3 T	low sodium or regular soy sauce
¼ t	pepper
½ t	sugar
1 T	sesame oil

Method:

1. Wash bok choy and cut into 1" sections. Separate the white parts from the green parts. Set aside.
2. Heat oil in a **nonstick** pan or wok; sauté onions and ginger root. Add ham and stir-fry for 1 minute.
3. Add tofu, the white parts of the bok choy, and the last 5 ingredients; bring to a boil. Turn to low heat and cook for 5 minutes.
4. Add the green parts of the bok choy and cook over high heat for 1 minute. Mix and serve. Makes 6 servings.

Fresh or Chinese dried mushrooms may be added to this dish.

Per serving:

Calories: 152	Fat: 13 gm (saturated fat = 15%)
Carbohydrates: 4 gm	Cholesterol: 14 mg
Protein: 7 gm	Sodium: 441 mg
Fiber: 1 gm	Calcium: 66 mg

MEAT-STUFFED FRIED TOFU

Ingredients:

½ lb   ground beef or pork
¼ C   water chestnuts, minced
¼ C   minced mushrooms
¼ C   minced onions
1 t   sherry
1 T   low sodium or regular soy sauce
1 t   minced ginger root
⅛ t   pepper
8 oz   Fried Tofu* (page 157)
3   green onions, cut into 1" long strips
2   slices ginger root
2 T   low sodium or regular soy sauce
1 t   brown sugar
1 C   water

Method:

1. Mix the first 8 ingredients together. This mixture will be the filling.
2. Slit an opening on the side of a piece of Fried Tofu; stuff with a teaspoon of the meat filling. Repeat the process until all the Fried Tofu pieces are stuffed.
3. Put the stuffed Fried Tofu pieces and the last 5 ingredients in a saucepan; bring to a boil.
4. Reduce to medium heat and cook until only a few tablespoons of water are left. Makes 6 servings.

This dish does not need constant attention while cooking.

The Fried Tofu can be kept for a few days in the refrigerator or several weeks in the freezer when wrapped in a plastic bag. The cooked, stuffed tofu can be made one or two days in advance. Heat in a pan before serving. Leftovers can be reheated and served.

*Fried Tofu is also available in Oriental grocery stores.

Per serving:

Calories: 145
Carbohydrates: 5 gm
Protein: 14 gm
Fiber: 1 gm

Fat: 8 gm (saturated fat = 4%)
Cholesterol: 27 mg
Sodium: 335 mg
Calcium: 83 mg

TOFU FOO YOUNG

Ingredients:

1lb	soft tofu
¼ lb	ground pork
¼ lb	shelled shrimp, fresh or frozen, minced
½ C	minced bamboo shoots
⅓ t	low sodium or regular salt
1 t	sherry
¼ t	pepper
¼ t	onion powder
½ t	sesame oil
3-4	Chinese dried mushrooms, soaked and shredded
⅓ C	finely shredded old fashioned ham (about 2 oz)
1-2	green onion, shredded
2	slices of ginger root, finely shredded
⅛ t	low sodium or regular salt
¼ t	pepper
1	egg white
1 t	sesame oil

Method:

1. Mix ground pork with the next 7 ingredients.
2. Place the tofu in a mixing bowl. Add the last 4 ingredients using a fork to break up the tofu. Mix thoroughly.
3. Put half of the tofu mixture in a deep heat-proof dish; add the pork mixture. Evenly spread the other half of the tofu on top of the pork. Gently press the surface until flat.
4. Spread the shreds of mushrooms, ham, green onion, and ginger root on top of the tofu. Steam in a steamer for 40 minutes. Serve hot. Makes 6 servings.

Per serving:

Calories: 140	Fat: 7 gm (saturated fat = 5%)
Carbohydrates: 4 gm	Cholesterol: 41 mg
Protein: 16 gm	Sodium: 265 mg
Fiber: 2 gm	Calcium: 98 mg

BRAISED-FRIED TOFU WITH SHRIMP

Ingredients:

¼ lb	shelled shrimp, fresh or frozen
⅛ t	low sodium or regular salt
¼ T	onion powder
⅛ t	pepper
1 t	cornstarch
2 T	corn or canola oil
6-8 oz	Fried Tofu* (page 157)
2	cloves of garlic, sliced
1 t	minced ginger root
2 C	water
1 t	low sodium instant chicken or vegetable bouillon
1 t	cornstarch blended with 2 T water
1 t	sesame oil
¼ lb	snow pea pods, cleaned
¼ lb	fresh mushrooms, washed and sliced
¼ t	pepper
2 T	or more, low sodium or regular soy sauce
1 t	sugar

Method:

1. Mix the shrimp with the next 4 ingredients. Set aside.
2. Heat 2 T oil in a **nonstick** pan. Stir-fry the shrimp for 1 minute. Remove.
3. Sauté ginger root and garlic in the remaining oil. Add water, chicken or vegetable bouillon, Fried Tofu and the last 4 ingredients; bring to a boil. Reduce to medium heat and cook for 5-8 minutes, or until juice is reduced to ¼ C.
4. Add 1 t sesame oil, snow pea pods, and blended cornstarch; cook and stir until the sauce thickens. Add cooked shrimp; mix well. Serve hot. Makes 6 servings.

*Fried Tofu is also available in Oriental grocery stores. It freezes well.

Per serving:

Calories: 103	Fat: 5 gm (saturated fat = 6%)
Carbohydrates: 6 gm	Cholesterol: 24 mg
Protein: 8 gm	Sodium: 255 mg
Fiber: 1 gm	Calcium: 76 mg

TOFU WITH PICKLED GREENS

Ingredients:

1 lb	firm or soft tofu, sliced (2"x1"x¾")
¼ lb	beef flank steak, sliced (2"x1"x⅛")
1 T	low sodium or regular soy sauce
¼ t	onion powder
¼ t	pepper
1 t	cornstarch
2-3 T	corn or canola oil
2	green onions, shredded
2	slices ginger root
⅙-¼	recipe of Pickled Mustard Greens (page 87), minced
½ t	sugar
	Salt and pepper to taste

Method:

1. Mix beef with the next 4 ingredients. Set aside.
2. Heat oil in a **nonstick** pan or wok. Add beef and stir-fry until color turns (1-2 minutes). Remove.
3. Add the onions and ginger root in the remaining oil and sauté for a few seconds.
4. Add tofu slices and the last 3 ingredients.
5. Turn to low heat; stir and cook for 2 more minutes. Add cooked meat; gently stir and mix well. Serve hot. Makes 6 servings.

One half to one teaspoon of sesame oil may be added before serving.

Per serving:

Calories: 137	Fat: 9 gm (saturated fat = 7 %)
Carbohydrates: 4 gm	Cholesterol: 13 mg
Protein: 11 gm	Sodium: 262 mg
Fiber: 2 gm	Calcium: 108 mg

SICHUAN TOFU

Ingredients:

- ½ lb ground pork or beef
- 1 T low sodium or regular soy sauce
- 1 t cornstarch
- 1 t sesame oil
- 2 t cornstarch blended with 2 T water
- 1 T corn or canola oil
- 2-3 T minced fermented (salted) black beans (see page 162)
- 1 T minced garlic
- 1 T minced ginger root
- 1 lb firm or soft tofu, diced
- ¼ t pepper
- 1-2 T low sodium or regular soy sauce
- ½ t Sichuan Peppercorn Powder for Dipping (page 90)
- 1 t Red Hot Pepper Oil (page 90)
- 1 t sugar
- ½ C water
- 1 t sesame oil (optional)

Method:

1. Mix the first 3 ingredients together thoroughly.
2. Heat oil in a **nonstick** pan or wok; add meat, black beans, garlic and ginger root. Stir and mix for 2-3 minutes, separating meat while stirring.
3. Add tofu and mix gently.
4. Add the last 7 ingredients; bring to a boil.
5. Add blended cornstarch and sesame oil; cook and stir until sauce thickens. Serve hot. Makes 6 servings.

Per serving:

Calories: 175
Carbohydrates: 5 gm
Protein: 15 gm
Fiber: 1 gm

Fat: 12 gm (saturated fat = 5%)
Cholesterol: 27 mg
Sodium: 264 mg
Calcium: 96 mg

BEAR'S PALM TOFU

Ingredients:

- 1 T low sodium or regular soy sauce
- ¼ t pepper
- ¼ t onion powder
- 1 t sherry
- 2 t cornstarch
- ½ lb chicken breast or pork
- ½ lb firm or soft tofu cut into 1½"x1"x½" slices
- 1 T cornstarch blended with 2 T water
- 1 t or more, sesame oil
- 2-3 T corn or canola oil
- 2 green onions, shredded
- 2 slices of ginger root
- ½ C washed, soaked, and shredded dried black wood ears
- 1-1½ C water
- 1-2 t low sodium instant chicken or vegetable bouillon
- 1-2 T low sodium or regular soy sauce
- ½ C bamboo shoots, sliced
- ½ t sugar
- ¼ t pepper

Method:

1. Slice the meat and mix with the first 5 ingredients.
2. Slice the tofu as directed.
3. Heat oil in a **nonstick** pan or wok; stir-fry the meat for 1½ minutes. Remove.
4. Brown both sides of the tofu slices with ginger root in the remaining oil. Add the last 7 ingredients; bring to a boil.
5. Add blended cornstarch and meat. Cook until the sauce thickens. Add sesame oil; mix well. Garnish with green onions. Makes 6 servings.

 A few snow pea pods can be added to the last step. Serve hot.

Per serving:

Calories: 170	Fat: 10 gm (saturated fat = 7 %)
Carbohydrates: 6 gm	Cholesterol: 22 mg
Protein: 16 gm	Sodium: 232 mg
Fiber: 2 gm	Calcium: 93 mg

MA LA TOFU

Ingredients:

1-2 T	corn or canola oil
½ C	ground pork or beef
1 t	or more, hot pepper flakes or cayenne pepper
1 t	finely minced ginger root
1 T	fermented(salted) black beans, minced (see page 162)
1 lb	firm or soft tofu, diced
2-3 T	low sodium or regular soy sauce
½ t	brown sugar
1 T	sherry
½ C	minced green onions
½ C	water
1 t	cornstarch blended with 2 T water
1 T	sesame oil
	Salt or soy sauce to taste
½ t	or more, Sichuan Peppercorn Powder for Seasoning (page 91)

Method:

1. Heat oil in a **nonstick** pan or wok; add meat. Stir and toss until color turns and meat particles separate.

2. Add hot pepper flakes, ginger root, and fermented (salted) black beans; stir and mix for 1 minute.

3. Add diced tofu, soy sauce, brown sugar and sherry; stir carefully for ½ minute.

4. Add green onions and water; mix and bring to a boil. Add blended cornstarch and sesame oil; cook until the sauce thickens. Transfer to a serving dish and sprinkle the Sichuan Peppercorn Powder over the tofu. Serve hot. Makes 6 servings.

This is a well known Western dish of the Sichuan province. It is famous not only for its hot and spicy flavor but also because it causes a tingling and numb sensation to the tongue. In Chinese, "Ma" means numb, the sensation from the Sichuan peppercorn powder, and "La" means hot, the flavor from the hot pepper. Ma and La are the two popular spicy flavors represented in most of the dishes from western China.

Per serving:

Calories: 169	Fat: 11 gm (saturated fat = 6 %)
Carbohydrates: 4 gm	Cholesterol: 27 mg
Protein: 15 gm	Sodium: 265 mg
Fiber: 1 gm	Calcium: 98 mg

TOFU WITH SMOKED FISH

Ingredients:

1 lb	soft tofu, sliced (2"x1"x¾")
¼ lb	smoked fish of your choice, soaked
2-3 T	corn or canola oil
4-6	green onions, shredded
4-6	slices of ginger root
1 t	cornstarch blended with 2 T of water
¼ t	pepper
1 t	sherry
½ t	sugar
1 C	water

Method:

1. Heat oil in a **nonstick** pan or wok; sauté the onions and ginger root.
2. Add smoked fish; stir for 1 minute.
3. Add tofu, and the last 4 ingredients. Cover and bring to a boil. Turn to low heat and cook for 8 minutes.
4. Add blended cornstarch and cook until the sauce thickens. Serve hot. Makes 6 servings.

Per serving:

Calories: 146	Fat: 11 gm (saturated fat = 10%)
Carbohydrates: 3 gm	Cholesterol: 15 mg
Protein: 11 gm	Sodium: 180 mg
Fiber: 1 gm	Calcium: 101 mg

SHRIMP TOFU

Ingredients:

¾ lb	firm or soft tofu, diced
¼ lb	shelled shrimp, fresh or frozen
1 t	sherry
⅛ t	onion powder
⅛ t	pepper
¼ t	low sodium or regular salt
2 t	cornstarch
2-3 T	corn or canola oil
2	green onions, minced
1 t	minced ginger root
2 t	cornstarch blended in ⅓ C water
½-1 C	washed, soaked and diced dried wood ears (see page 166)
¼ C	frozen peas, thawed
1-2 t	low sodium instant chicken or vegetable bouillon
½ C	water

Method:

1. Mix shrimp with the next 5 ingredients. Set aside.
2. Heat oil in a **nonstick** pan or wok; add shrimp and stir-fry until color turns (about 1-2 minutes). Remove to a dish.
3. Sauté green onions and ginger root in the remaining oil. Add tofu and the last 4 ingredients; stir for 1 minute.
4. Add blended cornstarch, cooked shrimp, and salt and pepper to taste. Stir and cook until the sauce thickens. Serve hot. Makes 6 servings.
   A few drops of sesame oil may be added before serving.

Per serving:

Calories: 121	Fat: 7 gm (saturated fat =7%)
Carbohydrates: 6 gm	Cholesterol: 24 mg
Protein: 9 gm	Sodium: 85 mg
Fiber: 2 gm	Calcium: 76 mg

TOFU MEAT BALLS

Ingredients:

½ lb	ground pork or beef
2	green onions, minced
½ T	minced ginger root
¼ t	pepper
1 t	sherry
2 T	low sodium or regular soy sauce
1-2 t	low sodium instant chicken or vegetable bouillon
1 t	sesame oil
6-8	water chestnuts, coarsely minced
1lb	firm tofu
2 T	cornstarch
	Sichuan Peppercorn Powder for Dipping (page 90)
	Oil for deep-frying
	Lettuce leaves (optional)
	Minced green onion or parsley for garnishing

Method:

1. Mix the first 10 ingredients together thoroughly using your hands. Add cornstarch and mix well.
2. Heat oil in a wok.
3. Form the tofu mixture into 1" balls and roll each one in cornstarch. Press to stick.
4. Deep-fry the balls until golden brown. Transfer to a lettuce-lined plate. Garnish with minced green onion or parsley. Serve hot with a small dish of Sichuan Peppercorn Powder for Dipping. Makes approximately 30 tofu balls.

Each Fried Tofu ball:

Calories: 46	Fat: 3 gm (saturated fat = 7%)
Carbohydrates: 1 gm	Cholesterol: 5 mg
Protein: 3 gm	Sodium: 42 mg
Fiber: 0 gm	Calcium: 18 mg

Calculated with 4 T oil for deep-frying

TOFU WITH BAMBOO SHOOTS

Ingredients:

¾ lb	firm or soft tofu, sliced (2"x1"x½")
1-2 oz	old fashioned dried ham, thinly sliced (2"x1"x⅙")
1-2 T	corn or canola oil
2	green onions, shredded
2	slices of ginger root
1 t	cornstarch blended with 2 T water
¾ C	sliced bamboo shoots
3-4	Chinese dried mushrooms, soaked and sliced
1 C	mushroom water
2 T	low sodium or regular soy sauce
⅛ t	pepper
1 t	sherry
1 T	sesame oil

Method:

1. Soak the dried mushrooms in 1½ C of hot water for 1-2 hours. Squeeze the soaked mushrooms dry and cut into slices. Save the mushroom water for later use.

2. Heat oil in a **nonstick** pan; sauté the onions and ginger root. Add sliced ham and stir-fry for one minute.

3. Add tofu and the last 7 ingredients and bring to a boil. Turn to low heat; cover and cook for 5 minutes.

4. Add blended cornstarch; cook and stir until the sauce thickens. Serve hot. Makes 6 servings.

Per serving:

Calories: 124	Fat: 9 gm (saturated fat = 12%)
Carbohydrates: 4 gm	Cholesterol: 7 mg
Protein: 7 gm	Sodium: 323 mg
Fiber: 2 gm	Calcium: 70 mg

MA PO TOFU

Ingredients:

1 lb	firm or soft tofu, diced
1-2 T	corn or canola oil
½ lb	ground pork or beef
1 T	minced garlic
2	green onions, minced
1 T	minced ginger root
¼ t	pepper
2-3 T	low sodium or regular soy sauce, divided
1 t	cornstarch blended with ¼ C cold water
½-1 t	Red Hot Pepper Oil (page 90) (optional)
½-1 t	Hot Pepper Sauce (page 92) (optional)
1 T	sesame oil

Method:

1. Mix meat with 1 T soy sauce and 1 t cornstarch.
2. Heat oil in a **nonstick** pan or wok. Add meat, minced garlic, onion, and ginger. Stir-fry for 1-2 minutes. Separate meat while stir-frying.
3. Add diced tofu, 1-2 T soy sauce and ¼ t pepper; stir and mix for ½ minute; salt to taste.
4. Cover pan and bring to a boil. Add water if tofu gets too dry.
5. Add well blended cornstarch, 1 T sesame oil, and Red Hot Pepper Oil and/or Hot Pepper Sauce, if desired. Stir and cook until sauce thickens. Serve hot. Makes 6 servings.

Per serving:

Calories: 171	Fat: 12 gm (saturated fat = 6%)
Carbohydrates: 3 gm	Cholesterol: 27 mg
Protein: 14 gm	Sodium: 306 mg
Fiber: 1 gm	Calcium: 96 mg

MEAT WITH TOFU GAN

Ingredients:

- ½ lb pork or beef, shredded
- 1-2 T low sodium or regular soy sauce
- ¼ t pepper
- 1 t sherry
- 1 t cornstarch
- ½ lb Tofu Gan,* shredded (page 157)
- 2 green onions, shredded
- 1 T shredded ginger root
- ½ C minced mustard greens, shredded carrots or shredded celery
- 1 t brown sugar
- 1 T low sodium or regular soy sauce
- 2-3 T corn or canola oil

Method:

1. Mix the first 5 ingredients together. Set aside.
2. Heat oil in a **nonstick** pan or wok; stir-fry meat until color turns. Remove and set aside.
3. Put Tofu Gan shreds, green onions, ginger root and 1 T soy sauce in the remaining oil; stir and mix for 3 minutes.
4. Add cooked meat, sugar, and mustard greens (celery or carrots). Stir and cook for 2 minutes. Serve hot. Makes 6 servings.

The leftovers can be reheated by stir-frying in a pan for a few minutes. Tofu Gan can be refrigerated for a few days or kept in the freezer for 2-3 months.

* Tofu Gan is also available in Oriental Grocery stores.

Per serving:

Calories: 159
Carbohydrates: 3 gm
Protein: 12 gm
Fiber: 1 gm

Fat: 11 gm (saturated fat = 6%)
Cholesterol: 27 mg
Sodium: 206 mg
Calcium: 77 mg

TOFU WITH FISH IN EARTHENWARE POT

Ingredients:

1 lb	fish head (any kind of large fish of your choice)
1 T	Sichuan Peppercorn Powder for Dipping (page 90)
1 T	cornstarch for coating
	Oil for deep-frying
1 in	ginger root, crushed
4	green onions, shredded
1T	sherry
1 t	pepper
¼ t	low sodium or regular salt, or to taste
1-2 oz	bean thread, soaked and drained
1 lb	firm or soft tofu, sliced (2"x1"x½")
1 t	low sodium instant chicken or vegetable bouillon
½ t	sugar

Method:

1. Wash the fish head (discarding the gills) and rub thoroughly, inside and out, with Sichuan Peppercorn Powder. Let it set
for 2 hours.
2. Coat fish head with cornstarch. Set aside.
3. Heat oil in a wok and deep-fry the fish head until brown
and crisp.
4. In an earthenware pot, add 2 cups of water, the fried fish
head, and the last 9 ingredients. Cover and bring to a boil. Turn
to low heat and simmer for 40 minutes. Serve hot in the same
earthenware pot. Makes 6 servings.

   One half to one teaspoon of sesame oil may be added before
serving.

   An earthenware pot is the authentic cookware for this dish
but any regular cooking pot can be used.

   Whole fish instead of fish head may be used in this recipe.

Per serving:

Calories: 172	Fat: 10 gm (saturated fat = 8%)
Carbohydrates: 7 gm	Cholesterol: 22 mg
Protein: 14 gm	Sodium: 260 mg
Fiber: 1 gm	Calcium: 107 mg

Calculated with whole catfish.

HOT TOFU

Ingredients:

1 lb	soft or firm tofu, diced
1-2 oz	steamed and minced old fashioned ham
2 t	cornstarch blended with 2 T of water
2 t	low sodium instant chicken or vegetable bouillon
1 C	water
1 T	sesame oil
1 t	or more, Hot Pepper Sauce (page 92)
2	green onions, minced
1 t	minced ginger root

Method:

1. Put the last 6 ingredients in a saucepan; bring to a boil.
2. Add the tofu and bring to a boil. Cover and cook over medium heat for 2 minutes.
3. Add blended cornstarch and cook until the sauce thickens.
4. Remove the cooked tofu to a serving dish. Sprinkle with minced ham and serve hot. Makes 6 servings.

One half to one teaspoon of sesame oil may be added before serving.

Per serving:

Calories: 101
Carbohydrates: 3 gm
Protein: 7 gm
Fiber: 1 gm

Fat: 7 gm (saturated fat = 10%)
Cholesterol: 3 mg
Sodium: 68 mg
Calcium: 83 mg

FERMENTED TOFU (TOFU LU) WITH MEAT

Ingredients:

2 lb	pork (butt, fresh ham, or shoulder, etc.)
4	pieces (1"x½" squares) fermented tofu (Tofu Lu) (see page 166)
3 T	Hoisin sauce
1 T	sherry
½ t	pepper
1	small onion, chopped
4	slices of ginger root
⅓ C	water

Method:

1. Cut the pork into 1½" cubes.
2. Place the fermented tofu, Hoisin sauce, sherry, and pepper in a small bowl and mash into a paste. Mix the paste with the pork. Let stand for 2 hours or more.
3. Put the last 3 ingredients in a medium saucepan. Add pork; cover and bring to a boil.
4. Reduce to low heat and cook for 1 hour or until the meat becomes tender and the liquid is reduced to ¼ C. Serve hot. Makes 6 servings.

Add more water if it evaporates before the meat becomes tender. If too much liquid remains after the meat is tender, turn up heat and cook until liquid evaporates.

Nutritional values of certain ingredients have not been analyzed; nutritional information for this recipe is not available.

main dishes
vegetarian

MAIN DISHES-Vegetarian

Baked Green Peppers with Tofu, 61
Black Bean Tofu, 82
Bon Bon Tofu, 73
Braised Fried Tofu, 89
Braised Tofu, 80
Chilled Mashed Tofu, 86
Cold Tofu, 86
Curried Tofu, 71
Five-Spice Juicy Tofu, 76
Fluffy Tofu, 72
Fried Tofu Balls, 79
Hot Pepper Sauce, 92
Meatless Tofu, 81
Mushroom Oyster Sauce Tofu, 66
Oyster Sauce Tofu, 83
Pan Fried Tofu, 84
Pickled Mustard Greens, 87
Pot Sticker Tofu, 77
Red Hot Pepper Oil, 90
Red Oil Tofu, 85
Sesame Paste, 91
Sichuan Chilled Tofu, 88
Sichuan Flavored Tofu Gan Shreds, 57
Sichuan Peppercorn Powder for Dipping, 90
Sichuan Peppercorn Powder for Seasoning, 91
Soy Sauce Fried-Tofu, 78
Spiced Tofu Gan, 75
Spicy Hot Sichuan Tofu, 67
Stir-Fry Tofu Gan with Vegetables, 63
Stir-fry Tofu with Vegetables, 60

Main Dish-Veg.

SICHUAN FLAVORED TOFU GAN SHREDS

Ingredients:

10 oz	Tofu Gan,* shredded (page 157)
¼ t	low sodium or regular salt
½ t	pepper
½ t	onion or garlic powder
2-3 T	corn or canola oil
1 T	finely shredded ginger root
4-5	green onions, shredded
½ C	shredded pickled pepper (Del Monte or other brand of yellow or green pickled peppers)
1 C	shredded bamboo shoots
1	carrot, shredded
1 T	sherry
1 t	honey
2-3	cloves of garlic, minced
¼-½ t	Sichuan Peppercorn Powder for Seasoning (page 91)
1 T	Red Hot Pepper Oil (page 90)
1 T	vinegar
1-2 T	low sodium or regular soy sauce
1 T	Hot Bean Paste (see page 161)
½ C	water
1 T	cornstarch

Method:

1. Place the last 10 ingredients in a bowl; blend well.
2. Heat oil in a **nonstick** pan or wok; sauté ginger root until brown.
3. Spread the Tofu Gan shreds evenly in the pan; sprinkle salt, pepper and onion powder over the Tofu Gan; fry until it is light brown and firm. Turn several times while frying.
4. Add onion, pickled pepper, bamboo shoots, carrots, and stir with the Tofu Gan for 1-2 minutes.
5. Add sauce mixture from step 1 and stir for 1-2 minutes. Serve hot with rice or bread. Makes 6 servings.

*Tofu Gan is also available in Oriental grocery stores.

Continued on next page

Per serving:

Calories: 149	Fat: 11 gm (saturated fat = 9%)
Carbohydrates: 8 gm	Cholesterol: 0 mg
Protein: 7 gm	Sodium: 353 mg
Fiber: 3 gm	Calcium: 96 mg

TOFU WITH GREEN PEAS

Ingredients:

1 lb	firm tofu
1-2 T	corn or canola oil
1 T	minced ginger root
1	medium onion, chopped
¼ t	low sodium or regular salt
½ t	pepper
½ t	garlic powder
1 T	Hot Bean Paste (see page 161)
1-2 T	low sodium or regular soy sauce
½ C	frozen green peas, thawed
2 t	cornstarch, blended with ½ C water
1 T	sesame oil

Method:

1. Cut tofu into 2"x2"x½" squares. Cut the tofu squares diagonally into triangles.
2. Heat oil in a **nonstick** pan or wok; sauté ginger root and onion until brown.
3. Spread the tofu in the pan and sprinkle salt, pepper, and garlic powder evenly over it. Fry the tofu for 1 minute, then turn and fry for another minute.
4. Add bean paste, soy sauce, and green peas and mix gently for 1 minute.
5. Add blended cornstarch and bring to a boil. Transfer the tofu to a serving dish; sprinkle sesame oil over it and serve immediately with rice or bread. Makes 6 servings.

Per serving:

Calories: 122	Fat: 8 gm (saturated fat = 9%)
Carbohydrates: 6 gm	Cholesterol: 0 mg
Protein: 8 gm	Sodium: 195 mg
Fiber: 2 gm	Calcium: 92 mg

TOFU WITH TOMATO AND SPINACH

Ingredients:

1 lb	firm tofu
½ lb	or more, fresh tomatoes
¼ lb	spinach, washed and drained
2-3 T	corn or canola oil
½ C	onion, minced, or 2-3 cloves of garlic, crushed
3	slices of ginger root
¼ t	low sodium or regular salt
2 T	low sodium or regular soy sauce
1 t	or more, sesame oil
1 t	cornstarch, blended with 1 T water

Method:

1. Cut the tofu into 2"x1"x½" slices. Cut the tomatoes into cubes. Break the spinach into small pieces.
2. Heat oil in a **nonstick** pan or wok; sauté onion and ginger root. Arrange the tofu slices in a pan in one layer. Sprinkle salt evenly on the tofu and brown.
3. Turn tofu and brown other side.
4 Add tomato and soy sauce; mix gently. Cover the pan and bring to a boil.
5. Add spinach, sesame oil, and blended cornstarch; cook until the spinach leaves are wilted. Serve hot with rice or bread. Makes 6 servings.

Per serving:

Calories: 127	Fat: 9 gm (saturated fat = 9%)
Carbohydrates: 6 gm	Cholesterol: 0 mg
Protein: 7 gm	Sodium: 270 mg
Fiber: 2 gm	Calcium: 109 mg

STIR-FRY TOFU WITH VEGETABLES

Ingredients:

2-3 T   corn or canola oil, divided

{ 1 lb   firm tofu, cut into 1"x1"x¾" pieces
2 T   low sodium or regular soy sauce
½ t   onion or garlic powder
¼ t   pepper
1 T   finely minced ginger root

½ C   sliced onion
1 t   finely shredded ginger root
Salt and pepper to taste

{ 1 C   water
2 t   cornstarch, blended with 1 T water
1-2 t   low sodium instant chicken or vegetable bouillon
2   stalks of broccoli
¼ lb   mushrooms, sliced
1 T   sherry

Method:

1. Heat 1-2 T oil in a **nonstick** pan or wok. Add the next 5 ingredients to the pan evenly. Brown both sides of the tofu. Remove.
2. Add 1 T oil, brown onion, and ginger root shreds.
3. Add the last 6 ingredients; bring to a boil.
4 Add the browned tofu, salt and pepper to taste, and stir gently for 1-2 minutes. Serve hot. Makes 6 servings.

Per serving:

Calories: 149
Carbohydrates: 7 gm
Protein: 8 gm
Fiber: 2 gm

Fat : 11 gm (saturated fat = 9%)
Cholesterol: 0 mg
Sodium: 216 mg
Calcium: 104 mg

BAKED GREEN PEPPER WITH TOFU

Ingredients:

- ½ lb   firm or soft tofu, crumbled
- 5-6   water chestnuts, chopped
- 1   green onion, minced
- ½ t   minced ginger root
- 1 T   low sodium or regular soy sauce
- 1 t   sherry
- ¼ t   pepper
- 1-2 t   low sodium instant chicken or vegetable bouillon
- 1-2 t   sesame oil
- 2 t   cornstarch
- 3-4   green peppers
-     Chili powder (optional)

Method:

1. Mix the first 10 ingredients in a bowl thoroughly.
2. Cut the green peppers into halves or quarters. Remove the stems and seeds.
3. Fill the green peppers with the tofu mixture; place the green peppers on a shallow tray and bake in a preheated 375° oven for 30 minutes. Sprinkle with a little chili powder before serving. Serve hot. Makes 6 servings.

Fresh mushrooms (with stems removed), tomatoes or any vegetable of your choice may also be used.

Per serving:

Calories: 59	Fat: 3 gm (saturated fat = 6%)
Carbohydrates: 6 gm	Cholesterol: 0 mg
Protein: 4 gm	Sodium: 106 mg
Fiber: 1 gm	Calcium: 47 mg

TOFU WITH SPINACH

Ingredients:

1 lb	tofu, sliced (2"x1"x½")
2	green onions, shredded
2	slices of ginger root
2-3 T	corn or canola oil
½ lb	fresh spinach
2 t	cornstarch blended with ¼ C of water
2 T	low sodium or regular soy sauce
⅛ t	pepper
½ C	water
¼ t	or more, sesame oil
2 t	low sodium instant chicken or vegetable bouillon
½ t	sugar

Method:

1. Wash spinach; drain well and cut into 1" sections.
2. Heat oil; sauté the onions and ginger root. Add tofu and the last 6 ingredients. Bring to a boil.
3. Turn to low heat; cover and cook for 5 minutes.
4 Add spinach; bring to a boil
5. Add blended cornstarch and bring to a boil. Serve hot.
Makes 6 servings.

Per serving:

Calories: 118   Fat: 9 gm (saturated fat = 9%)
Carbohydrates: 5 gm   Cholesterol: 0 mg
Protein: 7 gm   Sodium: 222 mg
Fiber: 2 gm   Calcium: 106 mg

STIR-FRY TOFU GAN WITH VEGETABLES

Ingredients:

- 2 T   low sodium or regular soy sauce
- ¼ t   pepper
- ¼ t   onion or garlic powder
- 1 T   minced ginger root
- 2-3 T   corn or canola oil
- 8 oz   Tofu Gan,* shredded (page 157)
- 1-2   carrots, shredded
- 1-2 T   low sodium or regular soy sauce
- ¼ lb   shredded spinach
- ¼ lb   bean sprouts
- 1 t   sugar
- 1 T   sesame oil

Method:

1. Heat oil in a **nonstick** pan or wok; add Tofu Gan shreds and the first 4 ingredients. Brown the Tofu Gan shreds.
2. Add carrot shreds and 1-2 T soy sauce and stir for 1-2 minutes.
3. Add the last 4 ingredients and stir for 1-2 minutes. Serve hot. Makes 6 servings.

   *Tofu Gan is also available in Oriental grocery stores.

Per serving:

Calories: 128
Carbohydrates: 6 gm
Protein: 6 gm
Fiber: 2 gm

Fat: 10 gm (saturated fat = 9%)
Cholesterol: 0 mg
Sodium: 324 mg
Calcium: 92 mg

TOFU GAN SALAD

Ingredients:

6 oz	Tofu Gan,* (page 157) cut into 1½"x½"x¼" pieces
2-3 T	corn or canola oil
	Fresh vegetables of your choice
	Salad dressing of your choice (pages 146-150)

$\left\{\begin{array}{l}\end{array}\right.$
2-3 T	low sodium or regular soy sauce
1 t	garlic powder
1 t	pepper
2 T	vinegar
1 t	honey

Method:

1. Heat oil in a **nonstick** pan or wok; add Tofu Gan pieces.
2. Spread the last 5 ingredients evenly on the Tofu Gan; brown the Tofu Gan on both sides. Cool. Makes 6 servings.

This browned Tofu Gan can be added to any of your favorite salads to increase the nutritional value and add a chewy texture. The browned Tofu Gan also can be used as a snack. It contains no cholesterol and is high in unsaturated fats.

*Tofu Gan is also available in Oriental grocery stores.

Per serving:

Calories: 83	Fat: 7 gm (saturated fat = 9%)
Carbohydrates: 3 gm	Cholesterol: 0 mg
Protein: 4 gm	Sodium: 203 mg
Fiber: 1 mg	Calcium: 52 mg

Vegetables are not included in this calculation.

TOFU GAN WITH CARROTS

Ingredients:

10 oz	Tofu Gan,* shredded (page 157)
½ lb	carrots, shredded
4-6	green onions, shredded
1 T	vinegar
2-3 T	corn or canola oil
1 T	shredded ginger root
¼ t	low sodium or regular salt, or to taste
½ t	pepper
1-2 T	low sodium or regular soy sauce
1-2 t	sesame oil

Method:

1. Heat oil in a **nonstick** pan or wok; sauté ginger root until brown.
2. Spread the Tofu Gan shreds evenly in the **nonstick** pan; sprinkle salt on Tofu Gan shreds; fry until the Tofu Gan turns brown. Turn several times while frying.
3. Add carrot shreds and soy sauce; stir for 2 minutes.
4. Add green onion shreds and stir for 1-2 minutes.
5. Add vinegar, sesame oil, and mix well. Serve hot with rice or bread. Makes 6 servings.

*Tofu Gan is also available in Oriental grocery stores.

Per serving:

Calories: 132	Fat: 10 gm (saturated fat = 9%)
Carbohydrates: 7 gm	Cholesterol: 0 mg
Protein: 7 gm	Sodium: 265 mg
Fiber: 2 gm	Calcium: 96 mg

MUSHROOM OYSTER SAUCE TOFU

Ingredients:

1 lb	firm or soft tofu, cut into ½" dices
½ C	water
1 t	cornstarch, blended with 2 T water
1-2 T	corn or canola oil
2-4	cloves of garlic, minced
1 t	or more, minced ginger root
1 T	minced ham (optional)
1	green onion, minced
¼ t	pepper
2-3 T	oyster sauce, or regular soy sauce
1 t	or more, hot sauce (optional)
1 T	sesame oil (optional)
½ lb	fresh mushrooms, diced
½ C	frozen green peas, thawed (optional)

Method:

1. Heat oil in a **nonstick** pan or wok; sauté garlic and ginger root.
2. Add tofu and the last 6 ingredients; cook for 1 minute. Stir gently while cooking.
3. Add water and bring to a boil.
4. Add blended cornstarch; mix well. Transfer to a serving dish; garnish with minced green onion. Sprinkle with ham and sesame oil, if desired. Serve hot. Makes 6 servings.

Per serving:

Calories: 103
Carbohydrates: 6 gm
Protein: 8 gm
Fiber: 2 gm

Fat: 6 gm (saturated fat = 7%)
Cholesterol: 0 mg
Sodium: 249 mg
Calcium: 94 mg

SPICY HOT SICHUAN TOFU

Ingredients:

1 lb	firm or soft tofu, diced
1 T	low sodium or regular soy sauce
2-3 T	corn or canola oil
1 T	minced ginger root
¼ lb	fresh mushrooms, chopped
¼ C	water chestnuts, chopped
3-4	green onions, minced
1 T	cornstarch
2 t	sugar
2-3	cloves of garlic, minced
1 T	Hot Bean Paste (see page 161)
1 T	sherry
½-1 t	Sichuan Peppercorn Powder for Seasoning (page 91)
1 T	or more, Red Hot Pepper Oil (page 90)
3 T	vinegar
1-2 T	low sodium or regular soy sauce
	Salt and pepper to taste

Method:

1. Mix the last 10 ingredients in a small bowl. Set aside.
2. Heat oil in a **nonstick** pan or wok; brown ginger root. Add tofu and 1 T soy sauce; stir gently and occasionally for 2 minutes.
3. Add chopped mushrooms and water chestnuts; stir gently for 2 minutes.
4. Add minced green onions and the sauce mixture from step 1 and stir for 1 minute. Serve hot. Makes 6 servings.

Per serving:

Calories: 153	Fat: 11 gm (saturated fat = 8%)
Carbohydrates: 8 gm	Cholesterol: 0 mg
Protein: 8 gm	Sodium: 237 mg
Fiber: 2 gm	Calcium: 95 mg

TOFU WESTERN (SICHUAN) STYLE

Ingredients:

- 1 T   sherry
- ½ t   Sichuan Peppercorn Powder for Dipping (page 90)
- ¼ t   onion powder
- ¼ t   pepper
- 1 lb   firm tofu
- ¼ C   flour
- 2   egg whites, lightly beaten
- 1 t   or more, sesame oil
- 2-3 T   corn or canola oil
- 1-2 t   low sodium instant chicken or vegetable bouillon dissolved in 1 C water, or 1 C chicken broth (page 16)
- 1 t   sherry
- 2   green onions, minced or 1 T minced garlic
- 1 t   minced ginger root
- 1 T   or more, Hot Bean Paste (see page 161)
- ½ t   sugar
- ¼ t   Sichuan Peppercorn Powder for Dipping (page 90)

Method:

1. Cut tofu into 1½"x1"x¼" pieces. Spread the first 4 ingredients evenly on tofu pieces. Let set for 10 minutes or more.
2. Coat the tofu pieces with a layer of flour and dip in egg whites before sautéing.
3. Heat oil in a **nonstick** pan or wok; sauté tofu pieces until both sides brown.
4. Add the last 7 ingredients to the tofu and bring to a boil. Turn to low heat and simmer until the cooking juice is reduced to ¼ C.
5. Add 1 t sesame oil and mix well. Transfer the tofu to a serving dish and serve hot. Makes 6 servings.

Per serving:

Calories: 122
Carbohydrates: 3 gm
Protein: 8 gm
Fiber: 1 gm

Fat: 9 gm (saturated fat = 9%)
Cholesterol: 0 mg
Sodium: 203 mg
Calcium: 87 mg

TOFU LION'S HEAD

Ingredients:

1 lb	firm tofu
3	slices of day-old bread, softened with water
¼ lb	fresh mushrooms, minced
4-5	water chestnuts, coarsely minced
1-2 t	pepper
⅛ t	Sichuan Peppercorn Powder for Dipping (page 90)
2-3 T	low sodium or regular soy sauce
1 t	minced ginger root
2	green onions, minced
1-2 t	low sodium instant chicken or vegetable bouillon
1 T	cornstarch
	Oil for deep-frying
2 C	water
1-2 T	low sodium or regular soy sauce
1 t	honey
½ lb	fresh mushrooms, sliced

Method:

1. Crumble the tofu into small pieces with a fork and squeeze it dry through two layers of cheesecloth. Squeeze the softened bread in the same manner.
2. Mix the first 11 ingredients together thoroughly. Divide the tofu into 4 portions. Form the 4 portions of tofu into 4 balls.
3. Heat oil for deep-frying. Fry the tofu balls until dark brown; drain.
4. Place the last 4 ingredients in a saucepan. Add fried tofu balls, cover pan and bring to a boil. Reduce to low heat and cook until the cooking juice is reduced to ½ C.
5. Transfer the tofu balls carefully to a serving dish. Pour the mushrooms and juice over the tofu balls and serve hot with rice or bread. Makes 6 servings.

Per serving:

Calories: 256	Fat: 14 gm (saturated fat = 7%)
Carbohydrates: 23 gm	Cholesterol: 0 mg
Protein: 14 gm	Sodium: 599 mg
Fiber: 4 gm	Calcium: 167 mg

Calculated with 2 T oil for deep-frying

TOFU WITH HOT BEAN PASTE

Ingredients:

1 lb	firm tofu, diced
1-2 T	corn or canola oil
3	green onions, minced
2-3 t	minced ginger root
3 T	Hot Bean Paste (see page 161)
¼ C	water
½ C	diced bamboo shoots
¼ lb	fresh mushrooms, sliced
1 T	sesame oil
	Minced parsley for garnishing

Method:

1. Heat oil in a **nonstick** pan or wok; sauté green onions and ginger root.
2. Add tofu, Hot Bean Paste and stir gently for 2 minutes.
3. Add bamboo shoots and water; stir and bring to a boil.
4. Add mushrooms and sesame oil; stir and cook for 1 minute. Transfer to a serving dish and garnish with minced parsley. Serve hot with rice or bread. Makes 6 servings.

Per serving:

Calories: 117	Fat: 9 gm (saturated fat = 9%)
Carbohydrates: 4 gm	Cholesterol: 0 mg
Protein: 8 gm	Sodium: 95 mg
Fiber: 2 gm	Calcium: 93 mg

CURRIED TOFU

Ingredients:

2-3 T	corn or canola oil
1 C	chopped onion
1 t	cornstarch blended with ¼ C water
1-2 T	curry powder blended with ¼ C water
½ lb	fresh mushrooms, diced
½ C	frozen peas
1 lb	firm or soft tofu, cut into ¾" dices
2-3 T	low sodium or regular soy sauce
¼ t	pepper
1 T	sherry

Method:

1. Heat oil in a **nonstick** pan or wok; brown onion. Add blended curry powder; stir and mix for 1 minute.
2. Add the last 4 ingredients; stir gently for 1-2 minutes.
3. Add mushrooms and peas; stir gently for 1-2 minutes.
4. Add blended cornstarch; cook until the sauce thickens. Serve hot with rice or bread. Makes 6 servings.

Per serving:

Calories: 134
Carbohydrates: 8 gm
Protein: 8 gm
Fiber: 3 gm

Fat: 9 gm (saturated fat = 7%)
Cholesterol: 0 mg
Sodium: 221 mg
Calcium: 96 mg

FLUFFY TOFU

Ingredients:

1 lb	firm tofu, crumbled
1-2 T	corn or canola oil
2-3	green onions, minced
1-2 t	finely minced ginger root
¼ lb	fresh mushrooms, chopped
½ C	chopped bamboo shoots or water chestnuts
¼ C	minced Sichuan pickle*
2 T	low sodium or regular soy sauce
1 t	honey
¼ t	pepper
1 T	sesame oil

Method:

1. Heat oil in a **nonstick** pan or wok; sauté onions and ginger root.
2. Add crumbled tofu and the rest of the ingredients; stir and cook until the tofu becomes dry and fluffy. Serve hot with rice, bread, oatmeal, or rice porridge. Makes 6 servings.

*Available in Oriental grocery stores.

Per serving:

Calories: 116
Carbohydrates: 5 gm
Protein: 7 gm
Fiber: 2 gm

Fat: 8 gm (saturated fat = 9%)
Cholesterol: 0 mg
Sodium: 341 mg
Calcium: 92 mg

BON BON TOFU

Ingredients:

1 lb	soft or firm tofu, diced into ¼" dices
2-3	green onions, minced
1 T	Sesame Paste (page 91)
2-3	cloves of garlic, minced
⅛-1 t	Sichuan Peppercorn Powder for Seasoning (page 91)
2 t	brown sugar
1 T	sesame oil
½-1 T	Red Hot Pepper Oil (page 90)
2 T	vinegar
2-3 T	low sodium or regular soy sauce
¼ t	pepper
1 T	oil (optional)
1-2 t	finely minced ginger root

Method:

1. Place the diced tofu and minced green onions on a serving plate.
2. Blend the rest of the ingredients thoroughly and pour this mixture over the tofu.
3. Mix gently before serving. Serve cold. Makes 6 servings.

Per serving:

Calories: 114
Carbohydrates: 5 gm
Protein: 7 gm
Fiber: 1 gm

Fat: 8 gm (saturated fat = 9%)
Cholesterol: 0 mg
Sodium: 207 mg
Calcium: 105 mg

SWEET AND SOUR TOFU BALLS

Ingredients:

1 lb	firm tofu
1	slice of day-old bread, soaked and squeezed dry
¼ lb	fresh mushrooms, minced
6-8	water chestnuts, coarsely minced
½ t	pepper
2-3 T	low sodium or regular soy sauce
2	green onions, minced
1 T	cornstarch
1 t	minced ginger root
½ T	sesame oil
	Flour for coating tofu balls, about 2 T

For Sauce:

½	green pepper, diced
¼ C	catsup
1 T	cornstarch
¼ C	honey
¼ C	vinegar
1 C	canned crushed pineapple
1 T	low sodium or regular soy sauce

Method:

1. Crumble the tofu into small pieces. Squeeze it dry through two layers of cheesecloth.
2. Mix the first 10 ingredients together thoroughly. Shape the tofu mixture into walnut-sized balls. Coat the balls with a layer of flour. Press to make sure the flour sticks to the balls.
3. Arrange the tofu balls on a tray. Bake in a preheated oven at 350° for 15-20 minutes.
4. For Sauce: Place all the ingredients, except the green pepper, in a saucepan; blend well. Bring the sauce to a boil, stirring constantly while cooking. Add green pepper; pour sauce over the baked tofu balls. Serve hot with rice or bread. Makes 6 servings.

Per serving:

Calories: 208
Carbohydrates: 32 gm
Protein: 9 gm
Fiber: 2 gm

Fat: 7 gm (saturated fat = 4%)
Cholesterol: 0 mg
Sodium: 475 mg
Calcium: 109 mg

SPICED TOFU GAN

Ingredients:

16 oz	Tofu Gan* (page 157)
½ t	five-spice powder (see page 163)
2 T	low sodium or regular soy sauce
1 C	water

Method:

Combine all the ingredients in a saucepan; cover and bring to a boil. Reduce to low heat and simmer for 20 minutes. Turn occasionally. If it becomes too dry while cooking, add a little water. Makes 4 servings.

To serve: Cut the tofu into small pieces; serve hot or cold as a main dish, snack or as one of the ingredients of many dishes.

*Tofu Gan is also available in Oriental grocery stores.

Per serving:

Calories: 135
Carbohydrates: 4 gm
Protein: 14 gm
Fiber: 2 gm

Fat: 8 gm (saturated fat = 7%)
Cholesterol: 0 mg
Sodium: 312 mg
Calcium: 186 mg

FIVE-SPICE JUICY TOFU

Ingredients:

1½ lb	firm tofu
	Oil for deep-frying
1 t	sesame oil
½-1 t	five-spice powder (see page 163)
1 t	onion powder
½ t	paprika
1 T	sherry
4-5 T	low sodium or regular soy sauce
3	slices of ginger root
2 T	honey
1½ C	water

Method:

1. Blend the last 8 ingredients in a saucepan; add sesame oil and bring to a boil.
2. Cut the tofu into 1"x1"x¼" slices. Dry the tofu slices with a towel.
3. Deep-fry the tofu until golden brown. Immediately transfer the fried tofu slices to the five-spice sauce. Let them soak in the sauces for 10-20 minutes, turning occasionally to get an even flavor.
4. Drain (reserve the sauce for later use). Serve either warm or cold, as a main dish, snack, or appetizer. Makes 6 servings.
   This juicy tofu can be frozen. Thaw before serving.

Per serving:

Calories: 167	Fat: 11 gm (saturated fat = 7%)
Carbohydrates: 10 gm	Cholesterol: 0 mg
Protein: 10 gm	Sodium: 409 mg
Fiber: 1 gm	Calcium: 131 mg

Calculated with 2 T oil for deep-frying and 2 T low sodium soy sauce.

POT STICKER TOFU

Ingredients:

1 lb	firm tofu
½ t	low sodium or regular salt
2-3 T	flour
1	egg white, lightly beaten
1 t	sesame oil
2-3 T	corn or canola oil
2	green onions, minced
1 t	minced ginger root
1 C	water
1 t	low sodium instant chicken or vegetable bouillon
¼ t	pepper
1 t	sugar
1 T	low sodium or regular soy sauce

Method:

1. Cut the tofu into ½"x½"x2" pieces and pat dry. Sprinkle the salt evenly over the tofu. Let stand for a few minutes or longer.
2. Roll the tofu pieces in the flour. Dip the tofu pieces, one at a time, in the beaten egg whites.
3. Heat oil in a **nonstick** pan or wok; fry the tofu on both sides until light brown. Transfer to a dish.
4. Sauté onion and ginger root. Add the last 5 ingredients and the fried tofu; bring to a boil.
5. Reduce to medium heat and cook until the liquid is reduced to ¼ C. Add sesame oil and mix gently. Serve hot. Makes 6 servings.

Per serving:

Calories: 124	Fat: 9 gm (saturated fat = 9%)
Carbohydrates: 5 gm	Cholesterol: 0 mg
Protein: 7 gm	Sodium: 161 mg
Fiber: 1 gm	Calcium: 86 mg

SOY SAUCE FRIED TOFU

Ingredients:

10 oz	Fried Tofu* (page 157)
2-3 T	low sodium or regular soy sauce
2	green onions, cut into 2" lengths
3	thin slices of ginger root
1 C	water
1 t	brown sugar

Method:

1. Put all the ingredients, except brown sugar, in a saucepan. Cover and bring to a boil.
2. Turn to low heat and simmer for 20 minutes.
3. Add brown sugar and cook over medium heat until only a few tablespoons of liquid are left. Serve hot or cold. Makes 6 servings.

One half to one teaspoon of sesame oil may be added before serving.

*Fried Tofu is also available in Oriental grocery stores. Most Oriental stores sell cooked and flavored Fried Tofu in cans which are imported from China or Japan. They are very delicious.

Per serving:

Calories: 94
Carbohydrates: 3 gm
Protein: 6 gm
Fiber: 1 gm

Fat: 7 gm (saturated fat = 9%)
Cholesterol: 0 mg
Sodium: 106 mg
Calcium: 85 mg

FRIED TOFU BALLS

Ingredients:

1 T	corn or canola oil
1	onion, chopped
1 T	finely minced ginger root
1 C	water
2 t	low sodium instant chicken or vegetable bouillon
8 oz	Fried Tofu* (page 157), cut into triangles
1 T	low sodium or regular soy sauce
1-2	thinly sliced carrots
1 t	cornstarch blended with 2 T water
½ C	freshly roasted nuts
2 C	broccoli flowerets
1 T	sesame oil

Method:

1. Heat oil; brown onion and ginger root.
2. Add the next 5 ingredients and bring to a boil. Turn to low heat and simmer for 5 minutes.
3. Add the last 3 ingredients; stir and bring to a boil. Add blended cornstarch; mix well. Serve hot. Makes 6 servings.

   *Fried Tofu is also available from Oriental grocery stores.

Per serving:

Calories: 189	Fat: 16 gm (saturated fat = 9%)
Carbohydrates: 8 gm	Cholesterol: 0 mg
Protein: 7 gm	Sodium: 19 mg
Fiber: 3 gm	Calcium: 92 mg

BRAISED TOFU

Ingredients:

1 lb	firm or soft tofu, diced
1-2 T	corn or canola oil
1 T	minced garlic
2 t	minced ginger root
1-2 t	low sodium instant chicken or vegetable bouillon
1-2 T	low sodium or regular soy sauce
¼ t	pepper
¾ C	water
1 t	cornstarch blended with 1 T water
1 T	Red Hot Pepper Oil (page 90) (optional)
1-2	green onions, minced
1 t	sesame oil

Method:

1. Heat oil in a **nonstick** pan or wok; sauté garlic and ginger root.
2. Add diced tofu, bouillon, soy sauce, and pepper; stir and cook for 2 minutes. Add water and blended cornstarch and bring to a boil.
3. Add Red Hot Pepper Oil, sesame oil, and mix well. Transfer to a serving dish and garnish with green onions. Serve hot with rice or bread. Makes 6 servings.

Per serving:

Calories: 115	Fat: 9 gm (saturated fat = 9%)
Carbohydrates: 3 gm	Cholesterol: 0 mg
Protein: 7 gm	Sodium: 207 mg
Fiber: 1 gm	Calcium: 88 mg

MEATLESS TOFU

Ingredients:

1 lb	firm or soft tofu, diced
1 t	sesame oil
1	green onion, minced
1-2 T	corn or canola oil
2	cloves of garlic, minced
2 t	minced ginger root
2 t	low sodium instant chicken or vegetable bouillon dissolved in 1 C hot water
¼ t	pepper
1 t	cornstarch blended with 1 T water
	Salt or soy sauce to taste

Method:

1. Heat oil in a **nonstick** pan or wok; sauté garlic and ginger root.
2. Add tofu; cook for 1 minute. Stir gently while cooking.
3. Add dissolved bouillon and ¼ t pepper; bring to a boil. Reduce heat and cook for 5 minutes. Add salt or soy sauce to taste.
4. Add blended cornstarch and mix well. Transfer to a serving dish. Garnish with sesame oil and minced green onions. Serve hot. Makes 6 servings.

Per serving:

Calories: 113	Fat: 9 gm (saturated fat = 9%)
Carbohydrates: 3 gm	Cholesterol: 0 mg
Protein: 6 gm	Sodium: 8 mg
Fiber: 1 gm	Calcium: 83 mg

BLACK BEAN TOFU

Ingredients:

1 lb	firm or soft tofu, diced
2-3 T	corn or canola oil
3-4 T	fermented (salted) black beans, minced (page 162)
3	slices of ginger root, finely minced
1-2 T	low sodium or regular soy sauce
3	green onions, minced
½ t	Hot bean paste (optional), (see page 161)
1 T	sesame oil

Method:

1. Heat oil in a **nonstick** pan or wok; sauté minced black beans and ginger root.
2. Add diced tofu and soy sauce; stir gently for 2-3 minutes.
3. Add the last 3 ingredients and stir gently for 1 minute.
Serve hot with rice or bread. Makes 6 servings.

Per serving:

Calories: 133	Fat: 11 gm (saturated fat = 9%)
Carbohydrates: 3 gm	Cholesterol: 0 mg
Protein: 8 gm	Sodium: 194 mg
Fiber: 1 gm	Calcium: 93 mg

OYSTER SAUCE TOFU

Ingredients:

1 lb	soft or firm tofu, diced
1-2 T	corn or canola oil
1 T	minced ginger root
2-3	finely minced green onions
2-3 T	oyster sauce or soy sauce
1 t	brown sugar
1 T	sesame oil
¼ t	pepper
¼ t	onion or garlic powder
1 t	sherry

Method:

1. Heat oil in a **nonstick** pan or wok; brown ginger root.
2. Add tofu and the last 6 ingredients; stir and cook for 2-3 minutes.
3. Transfer the cooked tofu to a serving plate. Garnish with green onions and serve hot. Makes 6 servings.

Per serving:

Calories: 107
Carbohydrates: 3 gm
Protein: 7 gm
Fiber: 1 gm

Fat: 8 gm (saturated fat = 9%)
Cholesterol: 0 mg
Sodium: 349 mg
Calcium: 86 mg

PAN FRIED TOFU

Ingredients:

¼ t	low sodium or regular salt
¼ t	onion or garlic powder
¼ t	pepper
1 lb	firm tofu
2 T	or more, flour
2-3 T	corn or canola oil
½ C	frozen peas, thawed
2-3	green onions, shredded
2-3	slices of ginger root
2 T	low sodium or regular soy sauce
1 t	honey
1 C	water

Method:

1. Mix the first 3 ingredients together in a small bowl.
2. Cut the tofu into 1½"x½" squares. Spread the salt mixture over the tofu evenly; let set for 1 hour.
3. Coat the tofu with a layer of flour.
4. Heat oil in a **nonstick** pan or wok; fry the tofu until brown on both sides.
5. Add the last 5 ingredients and cook until the cooking liquid is reduced to ¼ cup.
6. Add peas and mix well. Serve hot with rice or bread. Makes 6 servings.

Per serving:

Calories: 126	Fat: 8 gm (saturated fat = 8%)
Carbohydrates: 7 gm	Cholesterol: 0 mg
Protein: 7 gm	Sodium: 166 mg
Fiber: 2 gm	Calcium: 93 mg

RED OIL TOFU

Ingredients:

1 lb	firm tofu
1-2 T	corn or canola oil
1 T	minced ginger root
3-4	cloves of garlic, minced
1/8 t	or more, low sodium or regular salt
1/2 t	pepper
1-2 T	low sodium or regular soy sauce
1-2	green onions, minced
1 t	cornstarch blended with 1/3 C water
1-2 T	Red Hot Pepper Oil (page 90)

Method:

1. Cut tofu into 1½"x1½"x½" squares. Cut the tofu squares diagonally into triangles.
2. Heat oil in a **nonstick** pan or wok; sauté ginger root and garlic until brown.
3. Spread tofu in the pan; sprinkle 1/8 t salt and 1/2 t pepper evenly over the tofu. Fry the tofu for 1 minute then turn and fry the other side for another minute.
4. Add soy sauce and mix gently.
5. Add blended cornstarch and bring to a boil. Add Red Pepper Oil and mix gently. Transfer the tofu to a serving dish and garnish with minced green onions. Serve hot with rice or bread. Makes 6 servings.

Per serving:

Calories: 105	Fat: 8 gm (saturated fat = 9%)
Carbohydrates: 3 gm	Cholesterol: 0 mg
Protein: 6 gm	Sodium: 129 mg
Fiber: 1 gm	Calcium: 86 mg

CHILLED MASHED TOFU

Ingredients:

1 lb	chilled, soft tofu
2-3 T	low sodium or regular soy sauce
2 T	sesame oil
½ t	or more, Red Hot Pepper Oil (page 90)
2 T	vinegar
1 t	honey
¼ t	pepper
1 t	or more, finely minced ginger root
2	or more, green onions, minced
	Cilantro or parsley for garnishing

Method:

Mash all the ingredients except cilantro (or parsley) with a fork or a pair of chopsticks in a bowl until well blended. Garnish with chopped cilantro or parsley. Serve cold with rice or bread. Makes 6 servings.

Per serving:

Calories: 108	Fat: 8 gm (saturated fat = 9%)
Carbohydrates: 4 gm	Cholesterol: 0 mg
Protein: 7 gm	Sodium: 206 mg
Fiber: 1 gm	Calcium: 88 mg

COLD TOFU

Ingredients:

1 lb	soft tofu
2-3 T	low sodium or regular soy sauce
2	green onions, finely minced
1 t	minced ginger root
⅛ t	pepper
1 t	sherry
1 t	Hot Pepper Sauce (page 92) (optional)
2 T	sesame oil

Method:

1. Rinse the tofu and dry it with a paper towel. Cut tofu into dices and place in a bowl.
2. Add all the remaining ingredients to the diced tofu and mix well. Serve cold. Makes 6 servings.

Minced ham or soaked and minced Chinese mushrooms may be added.

Per serving:

Calories: 110	Fat: 9 gm (saturated fat = 10%)
Carbohydrates: 2 gm	Cholesterol: 0 mg
Protein: 7 gm	Sodium: 206 mg
Fiber: 1 gm	Calcium: 87 mg

PICKLED MUSTARD GREENS

Ingredients:

1 lb fresh mustard greens
1 T low sodium or regular salt

Method:

1. Wash mustard greens and let dry for half a day or overnight on a rack.
2. Put the mustard greens in a mixing bowl. Sprinkle salt evenly on the greens.
3. Mix and squeeze with your hands until the greens are wilted. Pack tightly in a glass jar. Keep in the refrigerator for 2 days before using. Makes 4 servings.

Pickled mustard greens can be used in many dishes. (See recipe on page 39).

The pickled greens can be stored in a covered glass jar in the refrigerator for as long as two weeks. Canned pickled greens may be purchased at Oriental grocery stores.

Per serving:

Calories: 30	Fat: 0.2 gm (saturated fat = 0.4%)
Carbohydrates: 6 gm	Cholesterol: 0 mg
Protein: 3 gm	Sodium: 853 mg
Fiber: 3 gm	Calcium: 120 mg

SICHUAN CHILLED TOFU

Ingredients:

1 lb	soft tofu, diced
4-6	green onions
1 T	sesame paste
2	cloves of garlic, minced
$\frac{1}{8}$ t	Sichuan Pepper Powder for Seasoning (page 91)
1 t	honey
1 t	or more, Red Hot Pepper Oil (page 90)
2 T	vinegar
$\frac{1}{4}$ t	pepper
1 T	sesame oil
2-4 T	low sodium or regular soy sauce
1 T	corn or canola oil
1 t	finely shredded ginger root

Method:

1. Place the diced tofu in a serving dish.
2. Wash the green onions; discard the green part and roots. Finely shred the white parts of the onions and spread over the tofu.
3. Mix the rest of the ingredients in a small bowl. Pour this mixture over the tofu. Mix gently before serving. Serve cold with rice or bread. Makes 6 servings.

Per serving:

Calories: 130	Fat: 10 gm (saturated fat = 9%)
Carbohydrates: 5 gm	Cholesterol: 0 mg
Protein: 7 gm	Sodium: 206 mg
Fiber: 1 gm	Calcium: 106 mg

BRAISED FRIED TOFU

Ingredients:

1 lb	Fried Tofu* (page 157)
3 C	water
3	green onions, minced
3	slices of ginger root
2-3 T	oyster sauce or soy sauce
1 T	sesame oil
	Salt to Taste
1 T	honey
¼ t	pepper
¼ t	ground hot pepper or cayenne powder (optional)

Method:

1. Place all the ingredients in a medium saucepan. Cover and bring to a boil.
2. Reduce to low heat and cook until cooking juice is reduced to ½ C. Serve with rice. Makes 6 servings.

*Fried Tofu is also available from Oriental grocery stores.

Per serving:

Calories: 157
Carbohydrates: 6 gm
Protein: 10 gm
Fiber: 2 gm

Fat: 11 gm (saturated fat = 8%)
Cholesterol: 0 mg
Sodium: 209 mg
Calcium: 136 mg

RED HOT PEPPER OIL

Place ¼ C of hot red ground pepper, pepper flakes or cayenne powder, 1 T Sichuan peppercorns and 1 t low sodium salt in a bowl. Heat 1 C oil in a pan or wok. Add a 1-inch piece of green onion and cook until the green part of the onion turns light brown.* Pour the hot oil over the pepper mixture and stir with a pair of chopsticks. Cover the bowl and let steep for 1 hour. The oil will turn red and have a Sichuan peppercorn aroma. This red oil is ready for use in your favorite dishes. It can be kept at room temperature for weeks. Makes 16 tablespoons.

*In China, this method is used to test the temperature of the oil. When the onion turns brown, the oil is the right temperature.

Per tablespoon:

Calories: 125
Carbohydrates: 1 gm
Protein: 0.2 gm
Fiber: 1 gm

Fat: 14 gm (saturated fat = 12%)
Cholesterol: 0 mg
Sodium: 71 mg
Calcium: 2 mg

SICHUAN PEPPERCORN POWDER FOR DIPPING

Heat a medium saucepan or wok over medium heat. Add ½ C Sichuan peppercorns; stir and turn for 2 minutes. Add ¼ C low sodium salt; stir and turn for 2 more minutes. Let cool. Place the cold, roasted peppercorns in a blender or food processor. Cover and blend into a fine powder, or crush the peppercorns with a mortar and pestle. Transfer the powder to a clean jar and keep at room temperature. The powder can be kept for months. Makes 12 tablespoons.

Nutritional information is not available for Sichuan peppercorns.

SICHUAN PEPPERCORN POWDER FOR SEASONING

Place ½ C Sichuan peppercorns in a blender or food processor. Grind the peppercorns into a fine powder. Transfer the powder to a container. The powder is now ready to use in your favorite dishes. This unroasted peppercorn powder gives the food not only a spicy flavor but also a "ma" (numb) feeling to the tongue. Makes 12 tablespoons.

The powder can be kept at room temperature for months.

Nutritional information is not available for Sichuan peppercorns.

SESAME PASTE

Ingredients:

  1 C   sesame seeds
  ¼ C   corn or canola oil

Method:

Spread 1 C sesame seeds in a tray. Roast the seeds in a preheated 300° oven for 12-15 minutes or until light brown. Or stir the sesame seeds in a wok over high heat until light brown. Allow the sesame seeds to cool. Place seeds in a blender or a food processor; grind the seeds into a paste. Add ¼ C of oil; mix well. Transfer the paste to a container and keep in the refrigerator. The sesame paste is ready for use in your favorite dishes. Makes 16 tablespoons.

Sesame seeds can also be ground with a mortar and pestle.

Per tablespoon:

Calories: 82	Fat: 8 gm (saturated fat = 11%)
Carbohydrates: 2 gm	Cholesterol: 0 mg
Protein: 2 gm	Sodium: 1 mg
Fiber: 1 gm	Calcium: 88 mg

HOT PEPPER SAUCE

Ingredients:

1 lb	fresh hot peppers, green or red
1 C	corn or canola
8-10	cloves of garlic
4	slices of ginger root
2-4	or more, fermented (salted) black beans (optional), (see page 162)
1 t	low sodium or regular salt
4-6	Chinese dried mushrooms, soaked and coarsely minced or ¼ lb fresh mushrooms (optional)
¼ C	dried shrimp, soaked and minced (optional)

Method:

1. Wash the hot peppers and discard the stems.
2. Cut the peppers in half, crosswise. Remove skin from garlic.
3. Place all the ingredients in a blender or a food processor and chop into fine particles.
4. Pour the pepper mixture into a deep saucepan (add mushrooms and shrimp); cover and bring to a boil. Reduce to low heat and simmer for ½ hour. Stir occasionally while cooking.
5. Transfer the cooked Hot Pepper Sauce to a clean jar and keep refrigerated. It is ready to use for your favorite recipes or as a dip with daily meals. Makes 40 tablespoons.

Hot Pepper Sauce can be frozen for 6 months. Thaw before using.

Per tablespoon:

Calories: 55	Fat: 6 gm (saturated fat = 11%)
Carbohydrates: 1 gm	Cholesterol: 0 mg
Protein: 0.4 gm	Sodium: 32 mg
Fiber: 0.2 gm	Calcium: 4 mg

a meal itself

A MEAL IN ITSELF

PAN-FRIED DUMPLINGS OR WONTONS

Ingredients:

15	wrapped dumplings or wontons (pages 19-22 for dumplings, pages 23-25 for wontons)
2-3 T	corn or canola oil
½ C	water

Method:

Spread oil in a **nonstick** skillet; arrange dumplings or wontons (without overlapping) in the skillet to cover the bottom. Add cold water; cover and bring to a boil. Turn to low heat and cook until water evaporates and a brown crust forms on the bottom of the dumplings. Remove the dumplings to a platter by turning the skillet upside down on the platter. Serve hot with a mixture of equal parts of soy sauce and vinegar.

Hot Pepper Sauce and minced garlic may also be added to the sauce.

Nutritional information for each uncooked Dumpling (page 20).
Nutritional information for each uncooked Wonton (page 23).

TOFU STEAK

Ingredients:

1 lb	firm tofu
2-3 T	flour
2-3 T	corn or canola oil
1-2 T	low sodium or regular soy sauce
1 T	or more, sherry
¼ t	pepper
½ t	onion or garlic powder
3	slices of ginger root or 1 T finely minced ginger root

Method:

1. Cut the tofu into 6 equal sized pieces. Towel dry.
2. Mix the last 5 ingredients in a shallow dish. Marinate the tofu in the sauce mixture for a few hours. Turn several times while marinating.
3. Sprinkle the tofu with a thin layer of flour. Heat oil in a **non-stick** pan; add tofu and fry until light brown and the tofu is heated. (Add marinade to pan while the tofu is cooking.) Makes 6 servings.

Serve hot with your favorite sauces, and with bread and a salad.

Per serving:

Calories: 88	Fat: 6 gm (saturated fat = 8%)
Carbohydrates: 3 gm	Cholesterol: 0 mg
Protein: 6 gm	Sodium: 106 mg
Fiber: 1 gm	Calcium: 83 mg

SLOPPY JOES

Ingredients:

2-3 T	corn or canola oil
6 oz	tomato paste
1 C	water
1 C	chopped onion
1 lb	firm tofu, crumbled
2-3 t	low sodium instant beef or vegetable bouillon
½ t	pepper
1 T	chili powder
1 t	ground cumin
1 t	sugar
1 C	minced celery
1	green pepper, diced
1 T	low sodium or regular soy sauce
2 t	oregano (optional)
½ C	grated carrot (optional)
½ C	sunflower seeds (optional)

Continued on next page

Method:

1. Heat oil in a **nonstick** pan or wok. Add all ingredients except tomato paste and water. Stir and cook for 5 minutes.
2. Add tomato paste and water; stir and cook for 3-5 minutes. Makes 6 servings.

Serve hot on buns and with a salad.

Per serving:

Calories: 87	Fat: 5 gm (saturated fat = 7%)
Carbohydrates: 10 gm	Cholesterol: 0 mg
Protein: 2 gm	Sodium: 152 mg
Fiber: 2 gm	Calcium: 30 mg

SPAGHETTI VERDE

Ingredients:

1-2 T	corn or canola oil
2	cloves of garlic, crushed
2-4	slices of ginger root
1	can (10 ¾ oz) cream of mushroom or cream of chicken soup
¼ C	water
½	recipe of Spiced Tofu Gan* (page 75) Tofu Gan Snack (page 138) or Fried Tofu* (page 157)
1	stalk fresh broccoli, cut into small pieces
3 oz	spaghetti, cooked

Method:

Heat oil in a pan; sauté garlic and ginger root. Add cream of mushroom (or cream of chicken) soup, water, and tofu. Bring to a boil. Add broccoli; stir and bring to a boil. Pour over cooked spaghetti and serve hot. Makes 6 servings.

*Tofu Gan and Fried Tofu are also available in Oriental grocery stores.

Per serving:

Calories: 173	Fat: 10 gm (saturated fat = 9%)
Carbohydrates: 16 gm	Cholesterol: 4 mg
Protein: 7 gm	Sodium: 228 mg
Fiber: 1 gm	Calcium: 97 mg

TOFU SPAGHETTI SAUCE

Ingredients:

2-3 T	olive oil
1 C	chopped onion
4-6	cloves of garlic, diced
6 oz	Fried Tofu,* diced (page 157)
½ C	sliced ripe olives
1	can (12 oz) tomato paste
3 ½ C	water
2 T	oregano
1 t	pepper
½ t	low sodium or regular salt
1 t	paprika
4	bay leaves
1 t	chili powder

Method:

1. Heat olive oil in a pan; brown onion and garlic.
2. Add the last 8 ingredients; blend well and bring to a boil. Turn to low heat and simmer for 5-8 minutes. Stir often.
3. Add Fried Tofu and cook for 2-3 minutes. Add olives before serving. Serve hot over cooked spaghetti. Makes 8 servings.
   If sauce is too watery, thicken with 1-2 t blended cornstarch.

   *Fried Tofu is also available at Oriental grocery stores.

Per serving:

Calories: 128	Fat: 8 gm (saturated fat = 8%)
Carbohydrates: 12 gm	Cholesterol: 0 mg
Protein: 5 gm	Sodium: 342 mg
Fiber: 3 gm	Calcium: 83 mg

SPICY TOFU BROIL

Ingredients:

1 lb	firm tofu
1 T	sherry
3-4 T	Hoisin sauce (see page 163)
1 T	low sodium or regular soy sauce
2 T	toasted sesame seeds
2-3	cloves of garlic, crushed and minced
1-2 t	minced ginger root
2 T	corn or canola oil

Method:

1. Cut the tofu into 4 equal pieces; towel dry.
2. Mix the rest of the ingredients in a bowl. Place the tofu in a shallow tray or cookie sheet. Spread half of the sauce mixture on the tofu.
3. Preheat the broiler. Place the tray 6" away from the broiler and broil tofu for 5-8 minutes.
4. Turn the tofu, spread on the rest of the sauce mixture, and broil for 5-8 more minutes. Serve hot with rice, noodles or bread and a salad. Makes 4 servings.

Per serving:

Calories: 112	Fat: 8 gm (saturated fat = 8%)
Carbohydrates: 4 gm	Cholesterol: 0 mg
Protein: 8 gm	Sodium: 189 mg
Fiber: 1 gm	Calcium: 118 mg

TOFU IN BARBECUE SAUCE

Ingredients:

1 lb	firm tofu
½ C	finely minced onion
¼ t	pepper
1 C	barbecue sauce of your choice
	Salt to taste

Method:

1. Cut the tofu into 4 equal pieces; towel dry and score. Arrange the tofu in a shallow tray in one layer.
2. Mix the rest of the ingredients in a bowl. Pour sauce evenly over the tofu; let it marinate for a few hours.
3. Preheat broiler. Place the tray of tofu 6" away from the broiler and broil for 8-10 minutes. Baste the tofu with sauce and broil for 8-10 minutes more. Serve hot with bread and a salad. Makes 4 servings.

Per serving:

Calories: 133 gm	Fat: 7 gm (saturated fat = 6%)
Carbohydrates: 10 gm	Cholesterol: 0 mg
Protein: 10 gm	Sodium: 518 mg
Fiber: 2 gm	Calcium: 138 mg

TOFU STROGANOFF

Ingredients:

1 lb	firm or soft tofu, crumbled
1-2 T	corn or canola oil
1	onion, chopped
1	can (10 ¾ oz) cream of mushroom soup
¼ C	water
	Salt and pepper to taste
	Cooked noodles or rice

Method:

1. Heat oil in a pan or wok. Sauté onion until brown.
2. Add crumbled tofu and stir for 1 minute.
3. Add cream of mushroom soup, water, and salt and pepper to taste. Stir and bring to a boil. Serve hot over noodles or rice. with a salad. Makes 6 servings.

Per serving:

Calories: 201	Fat: 9 gm (saturated fat = 9%)
Carbohydrates: 22 gm	Cholesterol: 4 mg
Protein: 9 gm	Sodium: 226 mg
Fiber: 2 gm	Calcium: 127 mg

CRUSTLESS TOFU QUICHE

Ingredients:

¾ lb	firm tofu, crumbled
½ C	milk
1 C	shredded cheddar cheese
1 C	chopped onion
¼ lb	fresh mushrooms, diced
5 oz	frozen, chopped spinach, thawed and squeezed dry
¼ t	curry powder
2-3 t	low sodium instant chicken or vegetable bouillon
½ t	pepper
¼ t	nutmeg
1 T	cornstarch
½ C	toasted almonds
	Salt to taste

Method:

1. Combine all the ingredients in a bowl; mix well.
2. Pour the tofu mixture into a pie pan; bake in a 375° oven for 35-45 minutes or until the surface turns light brown. Serve warm. Makes 6 servings.

This dish can also be made with a pie crust.

Per serving:

Calories: 169
Carbohydrates: 7 gm
Protein: 11 gm
Fiber: 2 gm

Fat: 11 gm (saturated fat = 24%)
Cholesterol: 20 mg
Sodium: 130 mg
Calcium: 227 mg

TACO TOFU

Ingredients:

{
1 lb	firm or soft tofu, crumbled
¼ t	onion or garlic powder
¼-½ t	ground cumin
½ t	oregano
1-3 t	chili powder
3 oz	tomato paste
	Salt and pepper to taste
1-2 T	corn or canola oil
10	taco shells
	For garnishing: Shredded lettuce, cheese, chopped tomato, onion, green pepper, avocado, and ripe olives. Taco sauce

Method:

1. Heat oil in a **nonstick** pan or wok; add the first 7 ingredients. Stir and cook for 3-5 minutes.

2. Spoon 2-3 tablespoons of the hot and seasoned tofu into each of the 10 taco shells. Place on a baking sheet and bake in a pre-heated 350° oven for 3-5 minutes.

3. Top taco shells with garnishings. Let your family create their own individual masterpieces. Makes 10 servings.

Per serving:

Calories: 114	Fat: 6 gm (saturated fat = 6%)
Carbohydrates: 12 gm	Cholesterol: 0 mg
Protein: 5 gm	Sodium: 74 mg
Fiber: 2 gm	Calcium: 79 mg

TOFU FRIED NOODLES

Ingredients:

- 1 T   minced ginger root
- ¼ t   pepper
- ¼ t   onion or garlic powder
- 2 t   low sodium instant chicken or vegetable bouillon
- 2-3 T   corn or canola oil
- 6 oz   Tofu Gan,* shredded (page 157)
- 1-2   carrots, shredded
- 1   onion, shredded
- 4 oz   noodles or thin spaghetti
- 2-3 T   low sodium or regular soy sauce
- ¼ lb   fresh spinach, shredded
- ¼ lb   bean sprouts
- 1 T   or more, sesame oil

Method:

1. Place the noodles (or spaghetti) in 2 to 3 quarts of rapidly boiling water; cook according to directions. Drain and rinse thoroughly under cold water.
2. Heat oil in a **nonstick** pan; add Tofu Gan shreds. Spread the first 4 ingredients evenly on the Tofu Gan and brown.
3. Add carrots, cooked noodles, soy sauce and onion; stir and cook for 3-5 minutes.
4. Add the last 3 ingredients and stir for 2-3 minutes. Serve hot as a meal or snack. Makes 6 servings.

   *Tofu Gan is also available from Oriental grocery stores.

Per serving:

Calories: 169	Fat: 9 gm (saturated fat = 7%)
Carbohydrates: 16 gm	Cholesterol: 0 mg
Protein: 7 gm	Sodium: 234 mg
Fiber: 3 gm	Calcium: 79 mg

MACARONI WITH TOFU

Ingredients:

1 lb	firm or soft tofu
1	clove of garlic
1 t	oregano
1 T	chopped parsley (optional)
½ t	pepper
2 T	corn or canola oil
1 T	vinegar
2 t	low sodium instant chicken or vegetable bouillon
1 C	frozen peas (optional)
½ lb	macaroni
2 T	olive oil or other oil (optional)
¼-½ C	grated parmesan cheese

Method:

1. Place the first 8 ingredients in a blender or food processor; blend until smooth and creamy.
2. Cook the macaroni according to the package directions.
3. Toss 2 T olive oil with the cooked and drained macaroni. Place the macaroni in a greased oven-proof dish; pour in tofu mixture and mix well.
4. Sprinkle parmesan cheese on macaroni and bake in a pre-heated 400° oven until the top is brown. Serve hot with a salad. Makes 6 servings.

Per serving:

Calories: 171	Fat: 9 gm (saturated fat = 9%)
Carbohydrates: 14 gm	Cholesterol: 3 mg
Protein: 9 gm	Sodium: 71 mg
Fiber: 2 gm	Calcium: 134 mg

CURRIED TOFU STRUDEL

Ingredients:

1 lb	firm tofu
1 T	minced ginger root
2 T	or more, curry powder
½ t	garlic powder or 1 t minced garlic
1	medium onion, minced
½ lb	fresh mushrooms, chopped
¼ t	pepper
2-3 T	low sodium or regular soy sauce
½ t	brown sugar
1 T	sherry
1 T	sesame oil
1 T	cornstarch
2 t	low sodium instant chicken or vegetable bouillon
	Oil for brushing (about 2 T) or butter
12	sheets of fillo dough

Method:

1. Dry the tofu with a towel and place in a bowl. Crumble the tofu into small pieces with a fork or with your hand.
2. Add all ingredients (except oil and fillo dough); mix well.
3. Place 1 fillo leaf on a damp towel. Brush top with oil. Place a second leaf over the first and repeat instructions. Place the third leaf over the second.
4. Spread ¼ of the tofu mixture along the edge closest to you. Lift the towel carefully so that the dough forms a roll. Fold the left and right ends under. Repeat to make 4 rolls.
5. Gently place the rolls on a greased cookie sheet or shallow tray, seam sides down. Brush top with oil or butter. Puncture the top of the rolls in several places with a toothpick.
6. Bake in a 350° oven for 30 minutes, or until the rolls turn light brown. Cut and serve while warm and serve with salad and bread. Makes 4 strudels.

I used ultra-thin "Apollo" fillo dough.

Per strudel:

Calories: 474	Fat: 17 gm (saturated fat = 4%)
Carbohydrates: 67 gm	Cholesterol: 0 mg
Protein: 21 gm	Sodium: 618 mg
Fiber: 4 gm	Calcium:151 mg

SPINACH TOFU STRUDEL

Ingredients:

1 lb	firm tofu
1 T	sesame oil
1 T	minced ginger root
1	medium onion, minced
¼ lb	fresh mushrooms, minced
1	box (10 oz) chopped frozen spinach, thawed and squeezed dry
2	cloves of garlic, minced
1-2 T	low sodium or regular soy sauce
1 t	chili powder
½ t	pepper
½ t	brown sugar
1 T	sherry
1 T	cornstarch
2 t	low sodium instant chicken or vegetable bouillon
	Oil for brushing (about 2 T) or butter
12	sheets of fillo dough

Continued on next page

Method:

1. Dry the tofu with a towel and place in a bowl. Crumble the tofu into small pieces with a fork or with your hand.
2. Add all the ingredients (except oil and fillo dough) to tofu and mix well.
3. Place 1 fillo leaf on a damp towel. Brush top with oil. Place the second leaf over the first and repeat instructions. Place the third leaf over the second.
4. Spread ¼ of the tofu mixture along the edge closest to you. Lift the towel carefully so that the dough forms a roll. Fold the left and right ends under. Repeat to make 4 rolls.
5. Gently place the rolls on a greased cookie sheet or shallow tray, seam sides down. Brush top with oil or butter. Puncture the top of the rolls in several places with a toothpick.
6. Bake in a 350° oven for 30 minutes, or until the rolls turn light brown. Cut and serve while warm. Makes 4 strudels.

Per strudel:

Calories: 485	Fat: 16 gm (saturated fat = 4%)
Carbohydrates: 69 gm	Cholesterol: 0 mg
Protein: 22 gm	Sodium: 684 mg
Fiber: 4 gm	Calcium: 243 mg

TOFU SPINACH SUPREME CASSEROLE

Ingredients:

1 lb	firm tofu, crumbled
1	box (10 oz) frozen spinach, thawed and squeezed dry
1 C	chopped onion
1	tomato, diced
2	cloves of garlic, minced
1-2 T	sesame oil
1	can (10 ¾ oz) cream of mushroom soup
½ t	pepper
¼ t	or more, curry powder
1-2 T	low sodium or regular soy sauce
2 C	cooked rice
½ C	sliced or slivered almonds

Method:

1. Mix all the ingredients, except almonds, in a bowl until well blended.
2. Transfer the tofu mixture into a shallow, greased baking dish; sprinkle the almonds evenly on top.
3. Bake, uncovered, in a 375° oven for 30-40 minutes or until the almonds are golden brown. Serve hot or warm. Makes 6 servings.

Cooked potatoes or macaroni can be used in place of rice.

Per serving:

Calories: 192
Carbohydrates: 11 gm
Protein: 11 gm
Fiber: 4 gm

Fat: 13 gm (saturated fat = 10%)
Cholesterol: 4 mg
Sodium: 266 mg
Calcium: 195 mg

TOFU SPINACH PIE

Ingredients:

2 lb	firm tofu, crumbled
2	boxes (10 oz) chopped frozen spinach, thawed and squeezed dry
1-2 T	corn or canola oil
¼ C	grated parmesan cheese
1 C	chopped onion
1-2 T	low sodium or regular soy sauce
½ t	pepper
2-3 t	low sodium instant chicken or vegetable bouillon
1 T	minced ginger root
1-2 t	minced garlic
1-2 t	sesame oil
2 T	cornstarch
1 T	sherry
12	sheets of fillo dough, fresh or frozen
	Oil or melted butter for brushing (about 2 T)

Continued on next page

Method:

1. Place all the ingredients (except fillo and oil for brushing) in a bowl; mix thoroughly.
2. Line a 9"x13" baking pan with a single sheet of fillo. This may be folded to fit the pan. Brush with oil or butter. Repeat this process until six sheets of fillo line the bottom of the pan. Spread the tofu mixture on the fillo. Use 6 fillo sheets on top of the tofu, buttering or oiling each piece (as with the bottom layer). Oil or butter top generously. Cut into squares. (An electric knife is helpful).
3. Bake for approximately 30-40 minutes at 350° until golden brown. Serve hot. Makes 12 servings.

Per serving:

Calories: 181   Fat: 8 gm (saturated fat = 7%)
Carbohydrates: 19 gm   Cholesterol: 1 mg
Protein: 11 gm   Sodium: 201 mg
Fiber: 3 gm   Calcium: 153 mg

TOFU MUSHROOM SUPREME CASSEROLE

Ingredients:

1 lb	firm tofu, crumbled
1 C	chopped onion
1-2	medium tomatoes, diced
1	box (10 oz) frozen peas, thawed
½ t	pepper
1-2 T	low sodium or regular soy sauce
1	can (10 ¾ oz) cream of chicken soup
2-3 T	sesame oil
½ lb	fresh mushrooms, diced
1 C	chopped broccoli
2 C	cooked rice, potatoes or macaroni
¼ C	grated cheese (optional)

Method:

1. Place all the ingredients in a bowl; mix thoroughly.
2. Transfer the tofu mixture into a shallow, greased baking dish. Bake, uncovered, in a 375° oven for 40 minutes or until the vegetables are soft. Serve hot or warm. Makes 6 servings.

Per serving:

Calories: 260	Fat: 11 gm (saturated fat = 8%)
Carbohydrates: 30 gm	Cholesterol: 6 mg
Protein: 13 gm	Sodium: 385 mg
Fiber: 6 gm	Calcium: 154 mg

TOFU FRIED RICE

Ingredients:

1 lb	firm tofu, diced
2 T	corn or canola oil
½-1 C	minced onion
2-3 t	low sodium instant chicken or vegetable bouillon
½ t	pepper
1 C	frozen peas and carrots
½ lb	fresh mushrooms, diced
2-3 C	cooked rice, hot
2-3 T	low sodium or regular soy sauce
1-2 T	sesame oil
2	green onions, minced

Method:

1. Heat oil in a **nonstick** pan, sauté onion. Add diced tofu, bouillon and pepper; stir and cook until the tofu dices turn brown.
2. Add mushrooms, peas and carrots; stir and cook until the peas and carrots are heated through (about 1 minute).
3. Add hot rice, soy sauce, and sesame oil; stir and mix well. Garnish with minced green onions. Serve hot. Makes 6 servings.

Continued on next page

Cooked pork, chicken or shrimp may be added to the rice at step 2.

Per serving:

Calories: 213   Fat: 11 gm (saturated fat = 6%)
Carbohydrates: 22 gm   Cholesterol: 0 mg
Protein: 10 gm   Sodium: 230 mg
Fiber: 3 gm   Calcium: 110 mg

TOFU RICE DELUXE, FRIED OR BAKED

Ingredients:

2-3 T	corn or canola oil
½ C	chopped onion
1-2 t	ginger root
1 lb	firm tofu, diced
2-3 C	hot cooked rice (page 114)
½ t	pepper
¼ lb	chopped mushrooms
1 C	frozen peas and carrots, thawed
½ C	diced bamboo shoots, water chestnuts, or green pepper (optional or all)
½ C	shredded or slivered almonds
2-3 t	low sodium instant chicken or vegetable bouillon
1-2 T	low sodium or regular soy sauce
1-2 T	sesame oil
¼ C	or more, grated parmesan cheese

Method:

1. Heat oil in a **nonstick** pan or wok; sauté onion and ginger root.
2. Add rest of ingredients; stir and cook for 5-8 minutes. Serve hot.
3. For baked rice: After step 1 of the method, add rest of the ingredients; blend well. Transfer to a baking dish and bake, covered, at 375° for 30 minutes. Uncover and bake for 10 more minutes. Serve hot. Makes 6 servings.

Per serving:

Calories: 269   Fat: 16 gm (saturated fat = 8%)
Carbohydrates: 22 gm   Cholesterol: 3 mg
Protein: 12 gm   Sodium: 194 mg
Fiber: 4 gm   Calcium: 171 mg

TOFU GAN CHOW MEIN

Ingredients:

- 1 T low sodium or regular soy sauce
- 1-2 t low sodium instant chicken or vegetable bouillon
- ¼ t pepper
- ¼ t onion or garlic powder
- 1 T finely minced ginger root
- 6-8 oz Tofu Gan,* shredded (page 157)
- 5 oz chow mein noodles
- 1-2 T corn or canola oil
- ½ lb celery cabbage, shredded, or bok choy, napa, spinach, etc.
- ¼ lb fresh mushrooms, shredded
- 1-2 carrots, shredded
- 1 T low sodium or regular soy sauce
- 2 t low sodium instant chicken or vegetable bouillon dissolved in 1½ C water
- 2 T cornstarch blended with 2 T water
- 2 green onions, shredded
- 1 T sesame oil

Method:

1. Heat oil in a **nonstick** pan or wok; add Tofu Gan shreds. Spread the first 5 ingredients evenly on the Tofu Gan and brown.
2. Add the last 8 ingredients; bring to a boil. Stir while cooking.
3. Place the chow mein noodles in a deep serving dish. Pour the Tofu Gan sauce on the noodles. Makes 6 servings.

Continued on next page

Serve hot as a meal or a snack.

*Tofu Gan is also available in Oriental grocery stores.

Per serving:

Calories: 204	Fat: 10 gm (saturated fat = 8%)
Carbohydrates: 22 gm	Cholesterol: 3 mg
Protein: 8 gm	Sodium: 450 mg
Fiber: 3 gm	Calcium: 73 mg

PLAIN RICE (FAN)

Ingredients:

    1 C   medium or long grain rice, enriched
    2 C   water

Method:

1. Place the rice and water in a small saucepan; cover and bring to a boil.
2. Remove lid; continue boiling over medium-high heat until water has completely evaporated.
3. Cover pan tightly. Reduce heat to lowest setting; simmer the rice for 20 minutes. Turn off heat but do not open lid until time to use the cooked rice. Makes 3 cups of cooked rice.
   Do not stir the rice or open the lid while simmering!
   If amount of rice is doubled, do not double the amount of water but add enough water to the pan to cover rice about 1".

If you follow the method faithfully, the result will be dry, fluffy rice with no mess and no rice stuck to the pan. This method of cooking rice is only good for small amounts (1-3 cups). When cooking larger amounts, the quantity of water should be readjusted.

Per cup of rice:

Calories: 223	Fat: 0 gm
Carbohydrates: 50 gm	Cholesterol: 0 mg
Protein: 4 gm	Sodium: 3 mg
Fiber: 1 gm	Calcium: 15 mg

desserts
& snacks

豆腐

DESSERTS AND SNACKS

COCONUT LEMON BARS

Ingredients:

Bottom layer:

½ C	frimly packed brown sugar
½ C	corn or canola oil
1 C	enriched all-purpose flour

Top layer:

1 lb	soft tofu
½-1 C	honey
¼ t	salt (optional)
2	egg whites
1 T	cornstarch
1	grated lemon peel from a fresh lemon
2 T	fresh lemon juice
1 C	flaked (shredded), sweetened coconut
¼-½ C	chopped walnuts

Method:

For bottom layer: Mix brown sugar and oil thoroughly in a
mixing bowl. Add flour and mix well to form a dough.
Press and flatten by hand to cover the bottom of an un-
greased 11½"x7½"x1½" pan. Bake in a preheated 375°
oven for 10 minutes.

For top layer: Place all the ingredients enclosed in bracket in a
mixing bowl; beat with an electric mixer until smooth (or use
a blender). Add coconut flakes and walnuts; mix well. Spread
the mixture evenly on the baked bottom layer. Bake in a preheated 375° oven for 35 minutes or until the top turns light
brown. Cool. Cut into bars before serving. Makes 3 dozen
bars.

Each bar:

Calories: 106	Fat: 5 gm (saturated fat = 11%)
Carbohydrates: 15 gm	Cholesterol: 0 mg
Protein: 2 gm	Sodium: 10 mg
Fiber: 1 gm	Calcium: 18 mg

WHOLE WHEAT PEANUT BUTTER COOKIES

Ingredients:

- 1 lb   soft tofu
- 2 T   corn or canola oil
- ½ C   sugar
- ½ C   firmly packed brown sugar
- 2   egg whites
- ½ C   peanut butter (low sodium or regular)
- 1 C   enriched all-purpose flour
- ½ C   whole wheat flour
- 1 t   baking powder
- 1 t   baking soda

Method:

1. Place the first 6 ingredients in a bowl and mix with an electric mixer until smooth.
2. Add the last 4 ingredients and mix with hands to form a smooth dough.
3. Form the dough into balls about 1" in diameter; flatten the balls into a ½" thickness. Place them 2 inches apart on a lightly greased cookie sheet.
4. Bake in a preheated 375° oven for 15-20 minutes. Makes 3 dozen cookies.

Per cookie:

Calories: 72
Carbohydrates: 10 gm
Protein: 2 gm
Fiber: 1 gm

Fat: 3 gm (saturated fat = 6%)
Cholesterol: 0 mg
Sodium: 48 mg
Calcium: 13 mg

WHOLE WHEAT SESAME COOKIES

Ingredients:

- 1 lb   soft tofu
- ½ C   corn or canola oil
- 1 C   firmly packed brown sugar
- 2 t   vanilla
- 2   egg whites
- 1 C   enriched all-purpose flour
- 1 C   whole wheat flour
- 1 t   baking powder
- 1 t   baking soda
- ¼-½ C   sesame seeds

Method:

1. Place the first 5 ingredients in a bowl and mix with an electric mixer until smooth.
2. Add the last 5 ingredients and mix to form a dough.
3. Drop the dough by the teaspoonful, about 2" apart, onto a lightly greased cookie sheet.
4. Bake in a preheated 375° oven for 20-25 minutes. Makes 3 dozen cookies.

Each cookie

Calories: 83	Fat: 4 gm (saturated fat = 6%)
Carbohydrates: 11 gm	Cholesterol: 0 mg
Protein: 1 gm	Sodium: 35 mg
Fiber: 2 gm	Calcium: 25 mg

WHOLE WHEAT ALMOND COOKIES

Ingredients:

- ½ lb   soft tofu
- ⅓ C   corn or canola oil
- 1 C   firmly packed brown sugar
- 2 T   almond extract
- 4   egg whites
- 1 C   all-purpose flour
- 1 C   whole wheat flour
- 1 t   baking powder
- 1 t   baking soda
- ½ C   almond slivers

Method:

1. Place the first 5 ingredients in a bowl and mix with an electric mixer until smooth.
2. Add the last 5 ingredients and mix by hand to form a smooth dough.
3. Form the dough into balls about 1" in diameter; flatten the balls into a ½" thickness. Place them 2 inches apart on a lightly greased cookie sheet.
4. Bake in a preheated 375° oven for 15-20 minutes. Makes 3 dozen cookies.

Each cookie:

Calories: 87	Fat: 4 gm (saturated fat = 5%)
Carbohydrates: 11 gm	Cholesterol: 0 mg
Protein: 2 gm	Sodium: 47 mg
Fiber: 1 gm	Calcium: 19 mg

PEANUT BUTTER HONEY BARS

Ingredients:
  Bottom layer:

  ½ C   frimly packed brown sugar
  ⅓ C   corn or canola oil
  1 C   enriched all-purpose flour

  Top layer:

  ½ lb   soft tofu
  ½ C   honey
  1 C   peanut butter
  2 t   vanilla
  2 T   cornstarch
  1 t   baking powder

Method:

  For bottom layer: Mix brown sugar and oil together. Add flour
    and blend well to form a dough. Press and flatten by hand
    to cover the bottom of an ungreased 11½"x7½"x1½" pan.
    Bake in a preheated oven at 375° for 8-10 minutes.
  For top layer: Place the ingredients for top layer in a mixing
    bowl and mix with an electric mixer until smooth (or use a
    blender). Spread the mixture evenly on the baked bottom
    layer. Bake in a preheated 375° oven for 35 minutes. Cool,
    then cut into bars. Makes 3 dozen bars.

Per bar:

Calories: 104	Fat: 6 gm (saturated fat = 8%)
Carbohydrates: 11 gm	Cholesterol: 0 mg
Protein: 3 gm	Sodium: 40 mg
Fiber: 1 gm	Calcium: 14 mg

SNOW WHITE BALLS

Ingredients:

1	recipe of Tofu Yogurt, plain (page 140)
¼-½ C	raisins
¼-½ C	chopped walnuts
1-2 C	coconut flakes

Method:

Blend tofu yogurt, raisins, and chopped walnuts in a mixing bowl. Place the coconut flakes in a shallow dish. Scoop up 1 tablespoon of the yogurt mixture and drop onto the coconut. Roll the yogurt mixture until coated with a layer of coconut. Repeat the process for the remainder of the recipe. Chill before serving. Makes 2 dozen balls.

Per ball:

Calories: 53
Carbohydrates: 4 gm
Protein: 2 gm
Fiber: 1 gm

Fat: 4 gm (saturated fat = 25%)
Cholesterol: 0 mg
Sodium: 12 mg
Calcium: 22 mg

TOFU BROWNIES

Ingredients:

10 oz	Pillsbury's "Lites Fudge Brownies" mix
1 lb	soft tofu
½ C	chopped walnuts or pecans (optional)

Method:

1. Place all the ingredients in a mixing bowl. With mixing spoon, stir until blended (batter will be heavy).
2. Spread into a lightly greased 9"x9"x2" baking pan. Bake in a preheated 350° oven for 25 to 30 minutes. Do not over bake. Cool thoroughly. Cut into squares before serving. Makes 24 brownies.

Each brownie:

Calories: 78	Fat: 3 gm (saturated fat = 3%)
Carbohydrates: 10 gm	Cholesterol: 0 mg
Protein: 2 gm	Sodium: 42 mg
Fiber: 0 gm	Calcium: 22 mg

SWEET SOY MILK WITH FRIED BISCUITS

Ingredients:

1-2	biscuits (ready-to-make, homestyle chilled biscuits, in tube)
1 C	hot soy milk (page 152 using step 5)
	Sugar to taste
	Oil for deep-frying, about 1 cup

Method:

1. Shape biscuits with hands into ½", sausage-like cylindrical rolls.
2. Heat oil in a wok; deep-fry the biscuits until brown.
3. Place the boiled hot soy milk in a soup bowl; add sugar. Cut the fried biscuits into 1" sections.
4. Add the biscuits to the hot soy milk and serve. Makes 1 serving.

Soy milk is sold in health food stores and most grocery stores.
In China, fried You Tiao with sweet soy milk is the nationally
popular breakfast. The fried biscuit here is a short cut for fried
You Tiao. The flavor and texture of fried biscuit and You Tiao
are very much alike.

Per serving:

Calories: 266	Fat: 19 gm (saturated fat = 10%)
Carbohydrates: 15 gm	Cholesterol: 0 mg
Protein: 11 gm	Sodium: 203 mg
Fiber: 2 gm	Calcium: 167 mg

Calculated with 2 teaspoons of oil for deep-frying.

WHOLE WHEAT DOUGH FOR STEAMED BUNS

Ingredients:

¼ oz	dry yeast (1 package)
¼-½ C	sugar
¼ C	all purpose flour
2 C	warm water
2 ¾ C	all purpose flour
2 C	whole wheat flour
1 T	baking powder
2-4 T	corn or canola oil

Method:

1. Mix yeast, sugar, and ¼ C flour in a large mixing bowl. Add
1 C warm water and blend well. Let stand for 15-20 minutes.
2. Add 1 C warm water to the yeast mixture; add the rest of the
ingredients. Mix well.
3. Cover the bowl with a kitchen towel and let rise until double
in bulk (about 1-2 hours, depending upon the temperature).
4. Place the dough on a floured board and knead for 5-8 minutes before using as wrappers for steamed buns (pages 126-129).

Whole recipe:

Calories: 2524	Fat: 36 gm (saturated fat = 2%)
Carbohydrates: 486 gm	Cholesterol: 0 mg
Protein: 71 gm	Sodium: 1006 mg
Fiber: 42 gm	Calcium: 334 mg

WHOLE WHEAT PEANUT BUTTER STEAMED BUNS

Ingredients:

½ lb	firm or soft tofu
½	recipe of Whole Wheat Dough (page 125)
24	2" squares of waxed paper
½ C	or more, peanut butter (low sodium or regular)
¼-½ C	firmly packed brown sugar
2 T	honey

Method:

1. Follow the recipe for Whole Wheat Dough (page 125, up to step 3).
2. Dry the tofu with a kitchen towel.
3. Add the last 3 ingredients to the tofu and blend thoroughly. This mixture will be the filling for the buns.
4. Divide the dough into 24 pieces. Flatten each piece of dough on a floured board with the palm of your hand. Roll each piece of dough into a 3" round wrapper. The center of the wrapper should be thicker than the edges.
5. Put 1 tablespoon of filling in the center of a wrapper. Gather all the edges together at the top; pinch the edges together and twist to make sure they are sealed.
6. Place each stuffed bun on a piece of waxed paper. Arrange the buns on tiers of a steamer (1" apart). Steam over boiling water for 15 minutes. Do not open the lid while steaming. Serve hot or warm. Makes 24 buns.

Cold steamed buns can be reheated by steaming over boiling water for 5-8 minutes or, wrap buns in a plastic sheet or bag and heat in a microwave oven (high setting) for ½ minute per bun before serving. The buns can also be frozen. To serve, thaw and reheat in a steamer or microwave oven.

Each bun:

Calories: 114	Fat: 4 gm (saturated fat = 5%)
Carbohydrates: 17 gm	Cholesterol: 0 mg
Protein: 4 gm	Sodium: 46 mg
Fiber: 1 gm	Calcium: 23 mg

WHOLE WHEAT SESAME PASTE STEAMED BUNS

Ingredients:

½ lb	firm or soft tofu
½	recipe of Whole Wheat Dough (page 125)
24	2" squares of waxed paper
½ C	Sesame Paste (page 91)
¼-½ C	firmly packed brown sugar
2 T	honey

Method:

1. Dry the tofu with a paper towel and crumble with a fork.
2. Add the last 3 ingredients to the crumbled tofu and blend thoroughly. This mixture will be the filling for the buns.
3. To wrap and steam the buns, follow steps 4-6 for Whole Wheat Peanut Butter Steamed Buns (page 126).
Makes 24 buns.

Cold steamed buns can be reheated by steaming over boiling water for 5-8 minutes or, wrap buns in a plastic sheet or bag and heat in a microwave oven (high setting) for ½ minute per bun before serving. The buns can also be frozen. To serve, thaw and reheat in a steamer or microwave oven.

Each bun:
Calories: 109   Fat: 4 gm (saturated fat = 4%)
Carbohydrates: 17 gm   Cholesterol: 0 mg
Protein: 23 gm   Sodium: 24 mg
Fiber: 1 gm   Calcium: 50 mg

VEGETARIAN'S STEAMED TOFU BUNS

Ingredients:

1 lb	firm tofu
½	recipe of Whole Wheat Dough (page 125)
1 C	firmly packed minced cilantro (coriander, or Chinese parsley)
2-3	green onions, minced
1 t	finely minced ginger root
2-3 T	low sodium or regular soy sauce
⅛ t	pepper
1-2 T	sesame oil
1 t	cornstarch
1 t	low sodium instant vegetable bouillon

Method:

1. Dry the tofu with a kitchen towel. Crumble the tofu with a fork.

2. Add the last 8 ingredients to the crumbled tofu and mix well. This mixture will be the filling for the buns. Makes 24 buns.

To wrap and steam the buns, follow steps 4-6 of recipe for Whole Wheat Peanut Butter Steamed Buns (page 126).

1 C minced mushrooms may be added or used as a substitute for the cilantro.

Cold steamed buns can be reheated by steaming over boiling water for 5-8 minutes or, wrap buns in a plastic sheet or bag and heat in a microwave oven (high setting) for ½ minute per bun before serving. The buns can also be frozen. To serve, thaw and reheat in a steamer or microwave oven.

Each bun:

Calories: 75	Fat: 2 gm (saturated fat = 4%)
Carbohydrates: 11 gm	Cholesterol: 0 mg
Protein: 3	Sodium: 73 mg
Fiber: 1 gm	Calcium: 32 mg

CHA SHAO TOFU STUFFED STEAMED BUNS

Ingredients:

8 oz	Fried Tofu* (page 157), cut into ¼" dices
½	recipe of Whole Wheat Dough (page 125)
24	2" squares of waxed paper
4-6 T	Hoisin sauce
6	or more, green onions, minced
1 T	finely mined ginger root
¼ t	pepper
1-2 T	sesame oil
2 T	water
1-2 T	low sodium or regular soy sauce
1 T	sherry

Method:

1. Mix the last 8 ingredients in a bowl and fold in the Fried Tofu. This mixture will be the filling for the buns.
2. Divide the dough into 24 pieces. Flatten each piece of the dough on a floured board with the palm of your hand. Roll each piece of dough into a 3" round wrapper. The center of the wrapper should be thicker than the edges.
3. Place 1 tablespoon of the filling in the center of the wrapper. Gather all the edges together at the top; pinch the edges together and twist to make sure they are sealed. Repeat for each bun.
4 Place each stuffed bun on a wax-paper square. Arrange them in tiers of a steamer about 1" apart. Steam over boiling water for for 15 minutes. Do not open the lid while steaming. Serve hot for lunch, as a snack, or as a whole meal. Makes 24 buns.

Cold steamed buns can be reheated by steaming over boiling water for 5-8 minutes or, wrap buns in a plastic sheet or bag and heat in a microwave oven (high setting) for ½ minute per bun before serving. The buns can also be frozen. To serve, thaw and reheat in a steamer or microwave oven.

*Fried Tofu is also available at Oriental grocery stores.

Continued on next page

Each bun:

Calories: 81

Carbohydrates: 11 gm

Protein: 3 gm

Fiber: 1 gm

Fat: 3 gm (saturated fat = 4%)

Cholesterol: 0 mg

Sodium: 75 mg

Calcium: 27 mg

TOFU GAN EGG ROLLS OR SPRING ROLLS

Ingredients:

½ lb	Tofu Gan* shredded (page 157)
¼ lb	leeks, finely shredded
1 oz	bean thread, soaked, drained, and cut into 1" sections
¼ lb	celery cabbage or napa, shredded
¼ lb	fresh mushrooms, shredded
¼ lb	bean sprouts
20	Egg roll skins
	Oil for deep-frying
1-2 T	corn or canola oil
1 T	finely shredded ginger root
¼ t	low sodium or regular salt
½ t	pepper
½ t	onion or garlic powder
2-3 T	low sodium or regular soy sauce
1 T	sherry
1 T	sesame oil
1-2 t	low sodium instant vegetable or chicken bouillon

Method:

1. Heat oil in a **nonstick** pan or wok; sauté ginger root until
brown.
2. Spread Tofu Gan evenly in the pan and sprinkle with salt,
pepper, and onion or garlic powder. Fry the Tofu Gan until
brown and firm. Turn several times while frying.
3. Add leeks, stir and mix for 2 minutes.
4. Add bean thread and the last 4 ingredients. Stir for 2 minutes.
5. Add celery cabbage, mushrooms, and bean sprouts; stir and
mix for 1 minute. Cool. This mixture is ready to use as egg roll
filling. Makes 20 egg rolls.
6. Put 1 tablespoon of filling on an egg roll skin and fold. (See
pages 133-135).
7. Heat oil for deep-frying. Fry the egg rolls until brown and
crisp. Serve hot with vinegar, a mixture of vinegar and soy
sauce, or Fruit Sweet and Sour Sauce (page 142).
8. To freeze: Lightly fry the egg rolls; cool. Line a container with
3 layers of paper towels. Place a layer of egg rolls on the towels
and cover them with 3-4 paper towels. Close container and
freeze. Thaw completely (in the container). Re-fry and serve.
Makes 20 egg rolls.

*Tofu Gan is also available in Oriental grocery stores.

Per egg roll:

Calories: 75	Fat: 4 gm (saturated fat = 6%)
Carbohydrates: 7 gm	Cholesterol: 0 mg
Protein: 2 gm	Sodium: 78 mg
Fiber: 1 gm	Calcium: 24 mg

SPINACH EGG ROLLS OR SPRING ROLLS

Ingredients:

1 lb	firm tofu
1-2 T	corn or canola oil
1 T	minced ginger root
½ lb	leeks, minced or 1 large onion, chopped
1-2 T	sesame oil
⅓ lb	fresh mushrooms, minced
1 C	chopped celery
1	box (10 oz) frozen chopped spinach, thawed and squeezed dry
20	egg roll skins and oil for deep-frying
	Oil for deep-frying

{
2-3 T	low sodium or regular soy sauce
½ t	pepper
1-2 t	low sodium instant vegetable or chicken bouillon
1 t	sherry

Method:

1. Crumble the tofu into small pieces.
2. Heat oil in a pan or wok; sauté ginger root until brown.
3. Add tofu, leeks, and the last 4 ingredients; stir and cook for 4-5 minutes.
4. Add sesame oil, fresh mushrooms, celery, and spinach; stir and cook for 1 minute. Cool. This mixture is ready to use as the egg roll filling.
5. To wrap: follow directions on pages 133-135.
6. To fry and serve: follow step 7 on page 131.
7. To freeze: follow step 8 on page 131.

Makes 20 egg rolls.

Each egg roll:

Calories: 79	Fat: 5 gm (saturated fat =7%)
Carbohydrates: 7 gm	Cholesterol: 0 mg
Protein: 3 gm	Sodium: 80 mg
Fiber: 1 gm	Calcium: 51 mg

Wrapping Egg Rolls:

1. With about one pound of Egg roll skins (wrappers) on a cutting board, trim off one corner.

2. With the trimmed corner opposite you, place a heaping tablespoon of cold filling across the upper part of the wrapper, spreading the filling into a 3½ "x1" portion.

3. Fold both uncut ends over the filling.

4. Roll the folded Egg roll up to within about 3" of the end.

5. Brush the end flap of the wrapper with a thin layer of seal made from a mixture of 1 T flour and ½ C water.

6. Finish rolling, making sure the sealing-brushed end is completely sealed.

Photographs by Sherl White

FRIED WONTON

Ingredients:

1 lb	firm tofu
3	green onions, finely minced
1-2 t	finely minced ginger root
2-3 T	low sodium or regular soy sauce
½ t	pepper
¼ t	garlic powder
1-2 T	sesame oil
½ C	firmly packed minced cilantro (Chinese parsley) or fresh mushrooms
70	wonton skins
	Oil for deep-frying

Method:

1. Crumble the tofu into small pieces with a fork.
2. Mix the tofu thoroughly with the next 7 ingredients.
3. Place 1 teaspoon of tofu mixture in the center of a wonton skin and fold up. (Instructions on pages 23-25)
4. Heat oil for deep-frying in a wok. Fry the wontons, a few at a time, until brown and crisp. Serve hot with vinegar, equal amounts of soy sauce and vinegar, or Fruit Sweet and Sour Sauce (page 142). Makes 70 wontons.

To freeze wrapped wontons: Arrange the wontons on a tray and keep in the freezer, uncovered, overnight. Carefully remove the frozen wontons and place in a plastic bag; seal and keep frozen. The frozen wontons can be kept for three months in the freezer. They can be used without thawing.

Per fried wonton:

Calories: 23	Fat: 1 gm (saturated fat = 6%)
Carbohydrates: 2 gm	Cholesterol: 0 mg
Protein: 1 gm	Sodium: 18 mg
Fiber: 0 gm	Calcium: 9 mg

Calculated with 3 T of oil for deep-frying.

TOFU TRIANGLES

Ingredients:

½ lb   firm tofu
1-2 T   corn or canola oil
1 t   minced ginger root
½ C   chopped onion
1 T   curry powder blended with 2 T water
1 t   cornstarch blended with 1 T water
1 T   sesame oil
30   wonton skins
   Oil for deep-frying
¼ lb   fresh mushrooms, minced
1-2 T   low sodium or regular soy sauce
¼ t   pepper
1 t   sherry
¼ t   paprika
1-2 t   low sodium instant vegetable or chicken bouillon

Method:

1. Dry the tofu and crumble into small pieces with a fork.
2. Heat oil in a **nonstick** wok; sauté ginger root until brown. Add chopped onion and blended curry powder; stir and cook for 2 minutes.
3. Add tofu and the last 6 ingredients; bring to a boil. Add sesame oil and blended cornstarch; mix well. Cool.
4. Place a portion of the curried tofu (about 2 t) in the center of a wonton skin. Fold the skin diagonally into the shape of a triangle. Seal the edges with water.
5. Heat oil for deep-frying. Fry the tofu triangles until brown and crisp. Serve with vinegar, equal amounts of soy sauce and vinegar, or Fruit Sweet and Sour Sauce (page 142), or eat plain. Makes 30 triangles.

Each triangle:

Calories: 36   Fat: 2 gm (saturated fat = 7%)
Carbohydrates: 3 gm   Cholesterol: 0 mg
Protein: 1 gm   Sodium: 21 mg
Fiber: 0 gm   Calcium: 11 mg

Calculated with 2 T of oil for deep-frying.

TOFU GAN SNACK

Ingredients:

12 oz	Tofu Gan,* (page 157) cut into 1"x1"x⅙" pieces
	Oil for deep-frying
2 C	water
2-3	slices of ginger root
2-3 T	honey
1-2 T	low sodium or regular soy sauce
¼ t	whole Sichuan peppercorns
½ t	garlic powder
⅛ t	low sodium or regular salt
¼ C	catsup
1	dried hot pepper

Method:

1. Heat oil; deep-fry the Tofu Gan until light brown. Drain.
2. Put the remaining ingredients in a pan or wok; cover and bring to a boil. Reduce to medium heat and cook for 1 minute.
3. Add the fried Tofu Gan; cover and bring to a boil.
4. Reduce to low heat and simmer until the liquid is reduced to 2 tablespoons. Turn several times during cooking. Serve hot or cold as a snack or as an entrée. Makes 6 servings.

*Tofu Gan is also available at Oriental grocery stores.

Per serving:

Calories: 143	Fat: 9 gm (saturated fat = 7%)
Carbohydrates: 11 gm	Cholesterol: 0 mg
Protein: 8 gm	Sodium: 348 mg
Fiber: 1 gm	Calcium: 97 mg

Calculated with 2 T of oil for deep-frying.

JADE RICE

Ingredients:

2 C	hot cooked rice (page 114)
1 lb	firm tofu, mashed
1 T	corn or canola oil
3	cloves of garlic, minced
¼-½ t	low sodium or regular salt, or to taste
1 C	or more, fresh parsley
1-2 T	olive oil
1-2 t	low sodium instant chicken or vegetable bouillon
1 T	or more, lemon juice

Method:

1. Place the parsley, olive oil, and lemon juice in a food processor or blender and blend into a paste. Set aside.
2. Heat oil in a **nonstick** pan or wok; sauté garlic. Add mashed tofu and salt; stir for 1-2 minutes.
3. Add rice and parsley mixture; stir and mix over low heat until well blended. Serve immediately. Makes 6 serving.

Per serving:

Calories: 167	Fat: 8 gm (saturated fat = 6%)
Carbohydrates: 17 gm	Cholesterol: 0 mg
Protein: 8 gm	Sodium: 59 mg
Fiber: 2 gm	Calcium: 106 mg

TOFU YOGURT

Ingredients:

1 lb	soft tofu
1 t	lemon juice
1-2 T	honey
1-2 T	corn or canola oil
½ t	vanilla

Choice of fruit preserves, marmalade, chopped nuts, fresh fruits, raisins, etc. (optional)

Method:

Place all the ingredients, except optionals, in a blender or in a food processor; blend until smooth and creamy. Add any of the items from the optionals. Serve chilled. The yogurt can also be frozen.

Makes 6 servings.

The tofu yogurt can be used in the following ways: As a filling for cream puffs, as a pie filling (sprinkle with some chopped nuts and nutmeg). As an ice cream (freeze yogurt first, then blend in a blender and refreeze). Use your imagination for addi tional ways to serve tofu yogurt.

Per serving:

Calories: 89	Fat: 6 gm (saturated fat = 8%)
Carbohydrates: 5 gm	Cholesterol: 0 mg
Protein: 6 gm	Sodium: 6 mg
Fiber: 1 gm	Calcium: 80 mg

Optionals are not included in this calculation.

TOFU WALNUT PUDDING

Ingredients:

¾ lb	soft tofu
1 C	walnuts
½ C	honey
2 C	water
1 T	vanilla
2 T	cornstarch blended with ¼ C water

Method:

1. Place the tofu and 1 C of water in a blender or in a food processor; cover and blend until smooth. Pour into a saucepan.
2. Place the walnuts in a blender or food processor; cover and blend for 1-2 minutes. Add to blended tofu; add 1 C of water. Stir and bring to a boil
3. Add honey and vanilla; stir and bring to a boil.
4. Add blended cornstarch; stir and bring to a boil. Serve hot, warm, or cold as a dessert or snack. Makes 6 servings.

Per serving

Calories: 245	Fat: 13 gm (saturated fat = 5%)
Carbohydrates: 30 gm	Cholesterol: 0 mg
Protein: 7 gm	Sodium: 7 mg
Fiber: 2 gm	Calcium: 77 mg

FRUIT SWEET AND SOUR SAUCE

Ingredients:

1 C	crushed peaches, apricots, orange segments, strawberries, or canned pineapple
2 C	water
6 T	honey
6 T	vinegar
1 T	cornstarch blended with 2 T water

Method:

Place all the ingredients except the blended cornstarch in a saucepan and bring to a boil. Add the blended cornstarch and bring to a boil. Stir while cooking. Serve warm or at room temperature with your favorite dishes as a sauce or dip.

Whole recipe:

Calories: 499
Carbohydrates: 136 gm
Protein: 2 gm
Fiber: 3 gm

Fat: 0 gm
Cholesterol: 0 mg
Sodium: 8 mg
Calcium: 21 mg

dips, spreads & dressings

DIPS

All the dips can be used as sandwich spreads or salad dressings. If they are too thick, dilute with one to two teaspoons of milk or soy milk.

ONION TOFU DIP

Ingredients:

½ lb	firm tofu
2 T	corn or canola oil
3-4 T	vinegar or lemon juice
⅓-½	package of onion soup mix (about 12-13 grams)

Method:

Place tofu, oil and vinegar (or lemon juice) in a blender or in a food processor. Blend until smooth. Transfer the tofu to a bowl and fold in the onion soup mix. Serve chilled.
The dip can be frozen.

Whole recipe:

Calories: 453 gm
Carbohydrates: 14 gm
Protein: 20 gm
Fiber: 3 gm

Fat: 39 gm (saturated fat = 10%)
Cholesterol: 0 mg
Sodium: 1092 mg
Calcium: 258 mg

CURRY TOFU DIP

Ingredients:

½ lb	firm tofu
2 T	corn or canola oil
3-4 T	vinegar or lemon juice
2 t	or more, curry powder
½ t	garlic powder
1-2 t	low sodium or regular instant chicken or vegetable bouillon
½ t	pepper

Method:

Place all ingredients in a blender or in a food processor. Blend until smooth and creamy. Serve chilled.

Whole recipe:

Calories: 450   Fat: 39 gm (saturated fat =10%)
Carbohydrates: 13 gm   Cholesterol: 0 mg
Protein: 19 gm   Sodium: 25 mg
Fiber: 4 gm   Calcium: 266 mg

CUCUMBER TOFU DIP

Ingredients:

½ lb	firm tofu
½	small cucumber
2 T	corn or olive oil
¼ C	low calorie Italian salad dressing
1-2 t	low sodium instant chicken or vegetable bouillon

Method:

Wash cucumber, remove the seedy portion. (Do not remove the skin). Cut the cucumber into small pieces. Place all the ingredients in a blender or in a food processor and blend until smooth and creamy. Serve chilled.

Whole recipe:

Calories: 477   Fat: 41 gm (saturated fat = 10%)
Carbohydrates: 14 gm   Cholesterol: 0 mg
Protein: 19 gm   Sodium: 497 mg
Fiber: 5 gm   Calcium: 260 mg

SESAME TOFU DIP

Ingredients:

½ lb	firm tofu
¼ C	toasted sesame seeds
⅓ C	low calorie or regular Italian salad dressing

Method:

Place all the ingredients in a blender or in a food processor. Blend until smooth and creamy. Serve chilled.

Whole recipe:

Calories: 421	Fat: 22 gm (saturated fat = 9%)
Carbohydrates: 17 gm	Cholesterol: 0 mg
Protein: 25 gm	Sodium: 649 mg
Fiber: 7 gm	Calcium: 590 mg

AVOCADO TOFU DIP

Ingredients:

½ lb	firm tofu
½ C	ripe avocado
1 T	vinegar or lemon juice
¼ C	low calorie or regular Italian salad dressing
2 t	low sodium instant chicken or vegetable bouillon

Method:

Place all the ingredients in a blender or in a food processor. Blend until smooth and creamy. Serve chilled.

Toasted and minced almonds or walnuts may be added after the tofu is blended.

Whole recipe:
Calories: 392
Carbohydrates: 20 gm
Protein: 20 gm
Fiber: 13 gm

Fat: 29 gm (saturated fat = 10%)
Cholesterol: 0 mg
Sodium: 409 mg
Calcium: 251 mg

JADE TOFU DIP

Ingredients:

¼ C	chopped fresh parsley or cilantro leaves
½ lb	firm tofu
2 T	corn or canola oil
2-4 T	vinegar or lemon juice
2-4 T	low calorie Italian dressing
2 t	low sodium or regular instant chicken or vegetable bouillon

Method:

Place all the ingredients in a blender or in a food processor. Blend until smooth and creamy. Serve chilled.

The dip can be frozen.

Whole recipe:
Calories: 462
Carbohydrates: 13 gm
Protein: 19 gm
Fiber: 4 gm

Fat: 39 gm (saturated fat = 10%)
Cholesterol: 0 mg
Sodium: 269 mg
Calcium: 260 mg

SWEET AND SOUR TOFU DIP

Ingredients:

½ lb	firm tofu
2 T	corn or canola oil
¼ C	vinegar or lemon juice
2 T	sugar
2 t	low sodium or regular instant chicken or vegetable bouillon
1-2 T	tomato paste
1 T	poppy seeds, slightly toasted (optional)

Method:

Place all the ingredients, except poppy seeds, in a blender or in a food processor. Blend until smooth and creamy. Add poppy seeds and mix well. Serve chilled.

Whole recipe:

Calories: 554
Carbohydrates: 40 gm
Protein: 19 gm
Fiber: 3 gm

Fat: 38 gm (saturated fat = 8%)
Cholesterol: 0 mg
Sodium: 38 mg
Calcium: 247 mg

making tofu

豆腐

TOFU MAKING

Ingredients:

> 1 C dried soybeans

Coagulants:

> ½ t calcium sulfate (natural gypsum) for soft tofu or,
> ½ t calcium chloride for firmer tofu.
> (2 T vinegar, 2 T lemon juice, 1 T Epsom salt, or 1½ t
> finely ground nigari dissolved in ½ cup of hot water
> can also be used as coagulants).

Method:

1. Wash and soak the soybeans in cold water overnight; drain. It will yield 3 cups of soaked soybeans.
2. Put a layer or two of clean cloth in a colander. Set the colander in a pan. Set aside.
3. In a food processor or blender. Blend half the soybeans into a paste; remove. Blend the other half of the soybeans in the same manner.
4. Place 6 cups of boiling water in a pan; add the soybean paste to the hot water and stir for 2-3 minutes.
5. Pour the soybean paste mixture into the cloth-lined colander (step 2). Squeeze the soy milk (the liquid) into the pan and discard the solids.
6. Boil the soy milk in a pan (I will call this pan, "pan A"). Stir the soy milk while cooking to prevent scorching. Keep on low heat and simmer for 1 minute.
7. Put the coagulant in another pan and add ½ cup of boiling water; stir to dissolve. (I will call this pan, "pan B").
8. Pour the boiling soy milk from pan A to pan B. Pour the soy milk back and forth between the two pans 2-3 times. Let it set for a few minutes. The soy milk will coagulate gradually.
9. Line a colander with 1-2 layers of clean cloth. Pour the coagulated soy milk into the colander. The coagulated tofu will remain on the cloth while the light yellow-colored, clear liquid (whey) will be strained away.
10. Gently press out the excess water from the tofu; cool. Remove the tofu and place it in cold water. The tofu is now ready to use.

Makes about ¾ pound of tofu.

If the soy milk does not coagulate after step 8, cook over medium heat until it coagulates; stir while cooking.

For one pound tofu:

Calories: 344	Fat: 22 gm (saturated fat = 8%)
Carbohydrates: 9 gm	Cholesterol: 0 mg
Protein: 37 gm	Sodium: 33 mg
Fiber: 6 mg	Calcium: 476 mg

Making Tofu:

Equipment needed for tofu making.

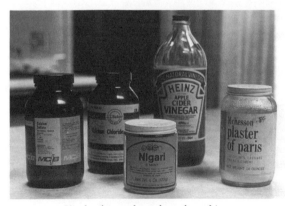

Kinds of coagulants for tofu making.

Tofu Making

Add blended soybeans to hot water, (step 4).

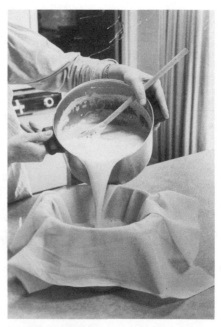

Pour soybean-paste mixture through cloth-lined colander, (step 5).

Squeeze soy milk from soybean mixture, (step 5).

Add coagulant to hot water, (step 7).

Pour boiling soy milk from pan A to pan B, (step 8).

Press out excess water from tofu, (step 10).

Finished tofu transferred to cold water.

Tofu
Making

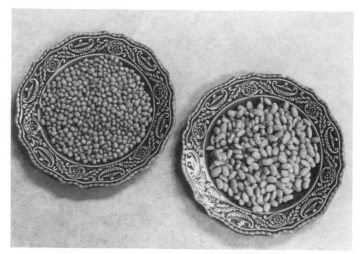

Dry soybeans and soaked soybeans.

Kinds of tofu.

Commercial tofu   Homemade tofu

Tofu gan

Fried tofu

HOMEMADE FRIED TOFU

Ingredients:

2 lb   fresh tofu
1-2 C   oil for deep-frying

Method:

1. Cut tofu into 2"x2"x1" pieces.
2. Towel dry the tofu pieces.
3. Heat oil in a wok. Fry tofu, a few pieces at a time until golden brown. Makes 20 ounces.

The Fried Tofu is ready to use. (See recipes on pages 12, 36, 38, 78, 79, 89, 99 and 129).

Fried Tofu can be kept frozen for 3 months. Fried Tofu can be bought in an Oriental grocery store by weight. Most Oriental grocery stores sell cooked and flavored Fried Tofu in cans. It is ready to eat.

Per ounce:

Calories: 53   Fat: 4 gm (saturated fat = 9%)
Carbohydrates: 1 gm   Cholesterol: 0 mg
Protein: 4 gm   Sodium: 3 mg
Fiber: 1 gm   Calcium: 48 mg

Calculated with 4 T of oil for deep-frying

HOMEMADE TOFU GAN (DRY TOFU)

Method:

Wrap 3 pounds of tofu in a large piece of cheesecloth. Put a cutting board or any flat article on the wrapped tofu. Add a heavy stone on top of the board and leave for several hours or overnight.

Continued on next page

Tofu
Making

Unwrap the cheesecloth. The Tofu Gan is ready to use in your favorite dishes. (See recipes on pages 48, 57, 63, 64, 65, 75, 104, 113, 130, and 138). Makes 32 ounces.

Tofu Gan can be purchased in Oriental grocery stores and tofu factories.

Per ounce:

Calories: 32
Carbohydrates: 1 gm
Protein: 3 gm
Fiber: 1 gm

Fat: 2 gm (saturated fat = 8%)
Cholesterol: 0 mg
Sodium: 3 mg
Calcium: 45 mg

ingredients

Ingredients, Seasonings, Storage and Substitutes

Bamboo shoots: New shoots of bamboo that sprout from the roots of mature plants. They are conical in shape and are eaten as vegetables. The ivory-colored edible portion is encased in many layers of husk. It has a fresh delicate vegetable taste. Mainly used for their crisp texture in a variety of dishes. Fresh bamboo shoots are occasionally available in the States. Canned bamboo shoots are sold in Oriental grocery stores and supermarkets. After opening the can, transfer the bamboo shoots to a clean, water-filled jar. Cover and store in the refrigerator for up to two weeks. Change the water once every two days. Bamboo shoots do not freeze well. Can be substituted by celery, cabbage stems, Chinese radishes, turnips, jicama, etc.

The mature bamboo plant symbolizes nobility and is loved by the Chinese. It is one of the "four gentlemen" of the Chinese floral world. (Others are chrysanthemums, plum flowers, and orchids). Bamboo plant stems probably have more uses than any other plant in Far Eastern countries.

Bean curd: See Tofu

Bean paste, hot: Fermented cooked soybeans; has a pungent, hot flavor. Used to enhance or heighten the flavor of meat, poultry, seafood, vegetable or noodle dishes. Sometimes it can be used to preserve cucumbers, eggplant, or cabbage. When diluted, it can be used as a table condiment and dip. Sold in cans in Oriental grocery stores. It can be kept for months in a clean jar after it is opened. Can be substituted by oyster sauce and mashed garlic.

Bean sprouts: The young sprouts of mung (green) beans or soybeans. Mung beans are more popular in America and easier to grow than soybean sprouts. They are used as vegetables in salads or in stir-fried dishes with shredded meat and other vegetables. Bean sprouts are sold fresh by weight or in cans in supermarkets or in Oriental grocery stores. They can be substituted by shredded cabbage stems or lettuce stems. I would not substitute canned bean sprouts for fresh ones. The texture and flavor are not the same. Bean sprouts can be grown at home. See *Nutrition and Diet with Chinese Cooking*, 7th edition, by Christine Liu, (recipe on page 185).

Bean threads (cellophane noodles, or Chinese vermicelli noodles): These opaque, fine noodles are made from ground green (mung) beans.

They are sold dried in bundles of 1-6 ounce packages in Oriental grocery stores or in some supermarkets. Must be soaked in warm water for half an hour and drained before using. After being soaked, noodles become soft, translucent and gelatinous. They easily absorb the flavors of other ingredients. Dried bean threads can be kept for a long time in a dry place.

Black beans, fermented (salted): These beans are called Dow See in Chinese. Small, cooked, fermented, and highly seasoned black soybeans that have a very strong, pungent flavor. Used to season meat, chicken and seafood. Sold in Oriental grocery stores in cans or plastic bags. After opening transfer to a tightly covered jar and store in the refrigerator. It will keep for months. Can also be frozen; thaw before using. Can be substituted by dark and thick soy sauce and mashed garlic.

Bok choy: see Chinese cabbage.

Broth or Stock: Good broth is the basis for soups, sauces, and liquid called for in various dishes. It is made from odds and ends of meat, poultry and bones through slow cooking or simmering. Strain broth through cheesecloth, discard the solids, then season with salt and spices. Good cooks, before MSG and bouillon were invented, always kept a pot of broth at hand to improve the flavor of various dishes. Can be substituted by canned chicken or beef broth or bouillon. (Recipe for Homemade Broth, page 16.)

Canola oil: Oil extracted from rape seeds. Canola oil has a healthy heart profile. It is the lowest in saturated fat of all the oils and second highest in monounsaturated fat, after olive oil.

Chinese cabbage: Celery cabbage, bok choy, and napa are collectively called cabbage in China. Celery cabbage has tightly packed stalks (leaves) somewhat resembling celery. Can be eaten raw for salad or stir-fried with meat and other vegetables. Bok choy has white, firm, loosely packed stalks and large dark green leaves and cannot be eaten raw. Napa has loosely packed, yellowish green wide leaves. Can be used exactly like celery cabbage. Sold fresh by weight in supermarkets.

Cumin: A flavoring agent for many foods. It is one of the principle ingredients of curry. It is not an authentic Chinese flavoring but I have adapted it to some of the new, creative tofu dishes.

Curry powder: A spice mixture originally from India. The Chinese adapted it centuries ago. Used in many chicken, meat and fish dishes. Sold in small jars or cans in the spice section of supermarkets. Also sold by weight in plastic bags in Oriental grocery stores.

Fermented (salted) black beans: See Black beans, fermented (salted)

Fermented tofu: See Tofu, fermented.

Fillo: Thin sheets of dough made from a mixture of wheat flour, water, cornstarch, salt, and vegetable oil. It is an important and basic ingredient in Greek cooking. Many well known dishes such as Baklava, Strudels, and pies etc. are made using fillo. I adapted it to new, creative tofu dishes in this book. It is sold frozen by the pound in many supermarkets in the frozen food section.

Five-spice powder or five-fragrance powder: Already mixed seasoning containing five ground spices: fennel, star anise, cloves, cinnamon, and Sichuan peppercorns. A small quantity is used in meat and poultry dishes. Sold by weight in Oriental stores. Can be kept in a dry place indefinitely. Allspice can be used as a substitute.

Garlic: Bulb of the garlic plant with a strong oniony aroma, used as seasoning in all types of dishes. A favorite seasoning of the Northern Chinese. (They sometimes eat it raw.) Sold in bulbs. Can be kept for months in a dry place. Leeks and onions can be substituted.

Ginger root, fresh: Brownish-skinned, gnarled, knobby, fibrous root of the ginger plant, about 2-3 inches long. Has a pungent, hot, spicy taste. Some people discard the ginger root after cooking before the food is served. It is a popular, all-purpose seasoning, and can be added to all types of dishes. The Chinese believe that ginger root aroma can cover up or neutralize unpleasant oders of fish, shrimp or meats, etc. Ginger root is used in a small amount by slicing, shredding, or mincing. When slices are called for in a recipe, they should be thin slices, cut across the grain about 1/8" thick. Ginger root doesn't have to be peeled before using, which will save time and reserve nutrients, but peeling before using is perfectly all right. The cut and peeled surfaces of ginger root mold easily. If this happens, cut off the molded surface and use the rest of the root. Sold by weight in most supermarkets, or in Oriental grocery stores. Keeps well for 2-3 weeks in the refrigerator wrapped in plastic. Can be substituted by dried ginger root (must be soaked before using). Never substitute with ginger powder.

Hoisin sauce: A thick, dark brownish-red paste made from fermented ground soybeans and spices. Has a sweetish spicy taste. Used in pork, poultry and seafood dishes, as well as for dipping. Sold in bottles or cans. After opening, transfer the sauce to a clean container or jar, cover and store in refrigerator. Can be kept for a year.

Lily buds or golden needles: Flower buds of lily plant, about 2-3 inches long. Freshly dried lily buds are pale gold-colored with a semi-soft texture. They turn brown and brittle when stored for a long period of time but this will not affect the flavor. Used as a vegetable in stir-fried, steamed or meat dishes, they impart a delicate flavor and chewy texture to the dish. Must be soaked 30 minutes in hot water and the hard stem removed (if there is any) before using. Sold dried by weight in packages. Can be kept in a dry place indefinitely. Fresh lily buds (the special edible kind) can be stir-fried and eaten as a vegetable.

Napa: See Chinese cabbage.

Oyster sauce: A thick, dark brown sauce made from soy sauce and oysters cooked together. It intensifies the flavor of meat, poultry and even vegetables. Used the same way as soy sauce. The oyster sauce is saltier and tastier. Reduce the quantity when substituting oyster sauce for soy sauce. Sold in cans and bottles in Oriental grocery stores. Will keep indefinitely in a cupboard.

Seaweed (dried purple vegetable) Zhi Cai: The most commonly used seaweed in soups, salads or as a garnish. It is conveniently prepared in the form of paper-thin, purplish-black sheets, each about 8 inches square and ready to add to dishes without cooking. It is rich in minerals. Sold in Oriental grocery stores by weight. Can be kept in a dry place for years.

Sesame oil: A strong, aromatic, nutty-flavored, amber-colored oil made from toasted sesame seeds. Used sparingly as flavoring. Adds a delicate taste to any dish. Absolutely not to be used for cooking. Sold in bottles or cans in different sizes in supermarkets or in Oriental grocery stores. Can be kept in well-sealed container in cupboard for one year.

Sesame paste: Made from toasted, ground sesame seeds. Has a strong, nutty flavor, but is different from "tahini" of Middle East. Used in salads, cold dishes or desserts. Sold in cans or bottles in Oriental grocery stores. Can be homemade (recipe on page 91). Will keep for months in the refrigerator.

Sesame seeds: Tiny, flat seeds used for garnishing as well as for flavoring on cookies, steamed cakes, candies or pastries. There are two kinds, black and white. Black ones are used mostly for garnishing. Sold in cans, jars, or loose by weight. Can be kept in a dry place indefinitely.

Sichuan peppercorn: A famous spice originating from Sichuan province. It looks like black peppercorn but is brownish in color and lighter in weight. It has a hollow shell outside and tough seed inside. Has a very pleasant aroma and mild hot flavor. Used in stir-fired, braised meat and poultry dishes. Also used in Sichuan pickles or as a table condiment when ground. Sold in Oriental grocery stores. Will keep indefinitely. No substitutes. Store Sichuan peppercorn in a basket (or similar container). Do not store in an airtight container or plastic bag. It will lose its flavor without proper air circulation.

Snow pea pods (sugar peas): Pale green, flat, crisp young pea pods. A special variety of Chinese origin. Grows very well in the mid-west in the summer. To cook, snap off both ends and stir-fry the whole pod. Only a short cooking time is needed to retain the tender, fresh taste and color. Sold year round in supermarkets. Fresh pea pods will keep for a week in the refrigerator in a plastic bag. Frozen pea pods are also available in 10 oz boxes and can be substituted for fresh ones.

Soy milk: The liquid extract from soaked and ground soybeans. It is the basic substance for making tofu (bean curd). Also used in other dishes. Very nutritious. Some people use it as a milk substitute if they are allergic to cow's milk. Can be homemade (see page 152, steps 5).

Soy sauce: A brownish, salty liquid made from a mixture of fermented cooked soybeans, flour and salt. It is an important and basic seasoning in Chinese cooking. An essential ingredient in 90% of Chinese dishes. A teaspoon of soy sauce contains about 342 milligrams of sodium. By comparison, a teaspoon of salt has about 2,000 milligrams of sodium. There is also a low sodium soy sauce available in most supermarkets; it has about half as much sodium as regular soy sauce. Tamari sauce can be used as a substitute.

Stock: See broth.

Tamari sauce: Tamari and soy sauce are similar but not the same thing. Tamari contains the same ingredients as soy sauce with the exception of wheat flour. Sodium content of tamari is 268 milligrams per teaspoon; flavor and richness are a bit different from soy sauce.

Tofu or bean curd: A highly nutritious vegetable protein made from soybeans. It has a smooth, custard-like texture and is ivory in color. Tofu itself is tasteless but easily absorbs the flavor of other food. It is a very delicate, fragile and perishable food and should be handled gently and with care. The Chinese consumption of tofu is comparable to the meat consumption of the Westerner. It is one of the most important sources of protein in the diet of the Chinese people. Tofu is sold fresh in squares (approximately one pound per square) in plastic containers or in cans; also can be homemade (recipe on page 152). It should be stored in a water-filled container in the refrigerator at all times. Change water once every two days. Can be kept for ten days.

Tofu Gan (dry tofu): Fresh tofu wrapped in cheesecloth and pressed (to reduce water content) into a semi-dry flat cake. Can be braised to make

165

spicy tofu to use as a snack. Sliced or shredded Tofu Gan is stir-fried with meat and vegetables. Sold in Oriental grocery stores or may be homemade (page 157).

Tofu, fermented, (Tofu Lu): Fresh tofu fermented with cultured bacteria, then seasoned with salt, spices and wine. The texture of fermented tofu resembles soft cheese. It is used with meat, fish, chicken and vegetable dishes, or served uncooked as a side dish. It is very popular in China when served with rice porridge in the morning as part of breakfast. Available in cans or jars. Can be kept in the refrigerator for months.

Tofu, fried: Deep-fried fresh tofu. It is light brown in color, with a crust-like texture outside; whitish and soft inside. Used in soups, braised with soy sauce and meat, or stuffed with ground meat and vegetables. Sold in Oriental grocery stores or can be homemade, (page 157). It is also sold in cans, cooked and flavored, and ready to eat.

Water chestnuts or Ma Ti: Literally "horse hooves" because of their shape and color. The plant grows in a water-flooded field. The edible portion is the root bulb of the plant, about one inch in diameter with a dark brownish skin and white meat. Fresh water chestnuts are available in Oriental grocery stores and some supermarkets. The young, tender water chestnuts are eaten as fruit. The mature ones are used as vegetables in stir-fried dishes, soups or in desserts. Canned water chestnuts are available in supermarkets and Oriental grocery stores. After opening canned water chestnuts, transfer them to a clean, water-filled jar, and store in the refrigerator up to three weeks. Change water once every two days. Never freeze water chestnuts. Peeled turnips or radishes can be substituted.

Wood ears, cloud ears, or tree fungus: Dried black, grayish, or dark brown, irregular shaped fungus which is grown on trees. After soaking, it expands 2-3 times its original size. Used in soups and stir-fried dishes. It adds a pleasant crunchy texture. Put in dishes at the last minute to assure crunchiness. There are many kinds of wood ears. Some are large and some are small. Sold in Oriental grocery stores by weight. Can be kept in a dry place indefinitely. Soak in warm water for at least 30 minutes and rinse before using. No substitutes.

Wood ears, white or silver snow ears: An opaque, cream-colored fungus. Larger than black wood ears. Softer in texture. After soaking, they can be used in stir-fry dishes just as black wood ears. Used in sweets and desserts. Sold in Oriental grocery stores.

References

Altschul, Aaron M.; *New Protein Foods*. Acadamic Press, New York, 1978

Bean, L.H.: *Closing the World's Nutritional Gap with Animal or Vegetable Protein*. FAO Bull. 6. 1966

Caliendo, Mary Alice: *Nutrition and the World Food Crisis*. Collier Macmillan Publishers, 1979

Chang, K.C.: *Food in Chinese Culture*. Yale University Press, New York. 1977

Ford, Barbara: *Future Food*. William Morrow and Company, New York, 1978

Lappe, F.M.: *Diet for A Small Planet*. Ballantine Books, Inc. N.Y. 1971

National Academy of Science: *Recommended Daily Dietary Allowances*. 8th, 1982

Smith and Circle: *Soybeans: Chemistry and Technology*. Volume 1. Proteins. The Avi Publishing Company, Inc. 1972

Untied States Department of Agriculture, Bureau of Human Nutrition and Home Economics: *Composition Of Foods Used In Far Eastern Countries*. Agriculture Handbook No. 34

United States Department of Agriculture, Home and Garden Bulletin: *Nutritive Value of Foods*. No. 72

United States Department of Agriculture, Agriculture Handbook: *Composition Of Foods, Raw, Processed, Prepared*. No. 8.

United States Department of Agriculture: *Nutritive Value of American Foods*. Agriculture Handbook No. 456

United States Department of Agriculture: *The Sodium Content of Your Food*. Home and garden Bulletin No. 233

Wike, Harold L.: *Soy Protein and Human Nutrition*. Academic Press, New York, 1979

Wolfe, W.J., et al: *Soybeans As A Food Source*. CRC Press, 1970

General Index

170

About the Author

Christine Liu is a native of Chongming, a large island, just outside of Shanghai—China's largest and most cosmopolitan metropolis. As a result, in her youth, she was able to experience not only traditional rural life, but also the various provincial tastes, customs, and cuisines which congregated in Shanghai. After her move to Taiwan, Christine attended National Taiwan University, where she received a degree in biology. While in college, she met and later married Dr. Stephen Liu, presently a professor of Microbiology at Eastern Michigan University.

After a short stay in Minnesota, the Lius moved to Sao Paulo, Brazil where they resided for several years. The Chinese community in that city was quite large, affluent, and diverse, with individuals from almost every province in China. The Lius quickly established themselves in the Chinese community. This afforded Christine the invaluable opportunity of supplementing her knowledge of Chinese cuisine by learning firsthand from experts in many regional Chinese food styles. These years in Brazil increased Christine's skill and expertise, and also aroused her latent talent and interest in the culinary arts.

The Lius returned to the United States in 1965, and have since resided in Ann Arbor, Michigan. In 1971, Christine received the M.P.H. degree in nutrition at the School of Public Health from the University of Michigan. She later did further graduate work at the Massachusetts Institute of Technology. After completing her education, Christine went about the task of using her education to teach nutrition and diet through Chinese cooking.

For more than a decade, Christine has taught subjects such as "Creative Chinese Cooking," and "Nutrition and Diet with Chinese Foods," and has coordinated classes in international gourmet cooking in the Continuing Education Department of the Ann Arbor Public Schools. Her most recent class is "Traveling and Eating in China," which is taught through the University Extension of the University of Michigan.

Her previous books, *Nutrition and Diet with Chinese Cooking*, and *More Nutritional Chinese Cooking*, have been very popular, with a combined total of seven printings. A now familiar figure on Michigan area television programs and in newspapers, Christine is a frequent lecturer on nutrition and demonstrator of Chinese food preparation. She is known for her enthusiastic advocacy of the nutritional qualities of Chinese food. Her expertise and enthusiasm has won her admiration and recognition among the public. For many years she has enjoyed a reputation of popularizing nutrition and diet with Chinese cooking.

Since normalization of relations between the United States and China, Christine has returned to her homeland many times. She was able to visit many famous restaurants and chefs in order to further deepen her knowledge of Chinese cuisine. During these trips, Christine was also able to travel to all parts of China and lecture at universities and to various groups about American food and culture.

In this, her latest book, Christine combines her experience in Chinese cuisine, along with many international styles, to bring her readers more nutritious recipes. She does this while centering her recipes around that originally Chinese invention—Tofu.